Cincinnati Reds 2020

A Baseball Companion

Edited by R.J. Anderson, Craig Goldstein and Bret Sayre

Baseball Prospectus

Craig Brown, Steven Goldman and David Pease, Consultant Editors
Robert Au, Harry Pavlidis and Amy Pircher, Statistics Editors

Copyright © 2020 by DIY Baseball, LLC.
All rights reserved

This book or any part thereof may not be reproduced or transmitted in any form or by any means, electronic or mechanical, including photocopying, recording, or by any information storage and retrieval system, without permission in writing from the publisher.

Limit of Liability/Disclaimer of Warranty: While the publisher and the author have used their best efforts in preparing this book, they make no representations or warranties with respect to the accuracy or completeness of the contents of this book and specifically disclaim any implied warranties of merchantability or fitness for a particular purpose. No warranty may be created or extended by sales representatives or written sales materials. The advice and strategies contained herein may not be suitable for your situation. You should consult with a professional where appropriate. Neither the publisher nor the author shall be liable for any loss of profit or any other commercial damages, including but not limited to special, incidental, consequential, or other damages.

Library of Congress Cataloging-in-Publication Data:
paperback
ISBN-13: 978-1-950716-00-5

Project Credits
Cover Design: Michael Byzewski at Aesthetic Apparatus
Interior Design and Production: Jeff Pease, Dave Pease
Layout: Jeff Pease, Dave Pease

Baseball icon courtesy of Uberux, from https://www.shareicon.net/author/uberux

Ballpark diagram courtesy of Lou Spirito/THIRTY81 Project, https://thirty81project.com/

Manufactured in the United States of America
10 9 8 7 6 5 4 3 2 1

Table of Contents

Statistical Introduction v

Part 1: Team Analysis

Cincinnati Reds: Where Are You Going, Where Have You Been? 3
    Zach Crizer, Keanan Lamb and Matthew Trueblood

Performance Graphs 7

2019 Team Performance 8

2020 Team Projections 9

Team Personnel 10

Great American Ball Park Stats 11

Reds Team Analysis 13

Part 2: Player Analysis

Reds Player Analysis 18

Reds Prospects 99

Part 3: Featured Articles

The Baseball Is Juiced (Again) 115
    Robert Arthur

The Moral Hazard of Playing It Safe 119
    Craig Goldstein

Index of Names 125

Statistical Introduction

Sports are, fundamentally, a blend of athletic endeavor and storytelling. Baseball, like any other sport, tells its stories in so many ways: in the arc of a game from the stands or a season from the box scores, in photos, or even in numbers. At Baseball Prospectus, we understand that statistics don't replace observation or any of baseball's stories, but complement everything else that makes the game so much fun.

What stats help us with is with patterns and precision, variance and value. This book can help you learn things you may not see from watching a game or hundred, whether it's the path of a career over time or the breadth of the entire MLB. We'd also never ask you to choose between our numbers and the experience of viewing a game from the cheap seats or the comfort of your home; our publication combines running the numbers with observations and wisdom from some of the brightest minds we can find. But if you *do* want to learn more about the numbers beyond what's on the backs of player jerseys, let us help explain.

Offense

We've revised our methodology for determining batting value. Long-time readers of the book will notice that we've retired True Average in favor of a new metric: Deserved Runs Created Plus (DRC+). Developed by Jonathan Judge and our stats team, this statistic measures everything a player does at the plate–reaching base, hitting for power, making outs, and moving runners over–and puts it on a scale where 100 equals league-average performance. A DRC+ of 150 is terrific, a DRC+ of 100 is average and a DRC+ of 75 means you better be an excellent defender.

DRC+ also does a better job than any of our previous metrics in taking contextual factors into account. The model adjusts for how the park affects performance, but also for things like the talent of the opposing pitcher, value of different types of batted-ball events, league, temperature and other factors. It's able to describe a player's expected offensive contribution than any other statistic we've found over the years, and also does a better job of predicting future performance as well.

There's a lot more to DRC+'s story, and you can read all about it in greater depth near the end of this book.

The other aspect of run-scoring is baserunning, which we quantify using Baserunning Runs. BRR not only records the value of stolen bases (or getting caught in the act), but also accounts for all the stuff that doesn't show up on the back of a baseball card: a runner's ability to go first to third on a single, or advance on a fly ball.

Defense

Where offensive value is *relatively* easy to identify and understand, defensive value is...not. Over the past dozen years, the sabermetric community has focused mostly on stats based on zone data: a real-live human person records the type of batted ball and estimated landing location, and models are created that give expected outs. From there, you can compare fielders' actual outs to those expected ones. Simple, right?

Unfortunately, zone data has two major issues. First, zone data is recorded by commercial data providers who keep the raw data private unless you pay for it. (All the statistics we build in this book and on our website use public data as inputs.) That hurts our ability to test assumptions or duplicate results. Second, over the years it has become apparent that there's quite a bit of "noise" in zone-based fielding analysis. Sometimes the conclusions drawn from zone data don't hold up to scrutiny, and sometimes the different data provided by different providers don't look anything alike, giving wildly different results. Sometimes the hard-working professional stringers or scorers might unknowingly inflict unconscious bias into the mix: for example good fielders will often be credited with more expected outs despite the data, and ballparks with high press boxes tend to score more line drives than ones with a lower press box.

Enter our Fielding Runs Above Average (FRAA). For most positions, FRAA is built from play-by-play data, which allows us to avoid the subjectivity found in many other fielding metrics. The idea is this: count how many fielding plays are made by a given player and compare that to expected plays for an average fielder at their position (based on pitcher ground ball tendencies and batter handedness). Then we adjust for park and base-out situations.

When it comes to catchers, our methodology is a little different thanks to the laundry list of responsibilities they're tasked with beyond just, well, catching and throwing the ball. By now you've probably heard about "framing" or the art of making umpires more likely to call balls outside the strike zone for strikes. To put this into one tidy number, we incorporate pitch tracking data (for the years it exists) and adjust for important factors like pitcher, umpire, batter and home-field advantage using a mixed-model approach. This grants us a number for how many strikes the catcher is personally adding to (or subtracting from) his pitchers' performance...which we then convert to runs added or lost using linear weights.

Framing is one of the biggest parts of determining catcher value, but we also take into account blocking balls from going past, whether a scorer deems it a passed ball or a wild pitch. We use a similar approach—one that really benefits from the pitch tracking data that tells us what ends up in the dirt and what doesn't. We also include a catcher's ability to prevent stolen bases and how well they field balls in play, and *finally* we come up with our FRAA for catchers.

Pitching

Both pitching and fielding make up the half of baseball that isn't run scoring: run prevention. Separating pitching from fielding is a tough task, and most recent pitching analysis has branched off from Voros McCracken's famous (and controversial) statement, "There is little if any difference among major-league pitchers in their ability to prevent hits on balls hit in the field of play." The research of the analytic community has validated this to some extent, and there are a host of "defense-independent" pitching measures that have been developed to try and extract the effect of the defense behind a hurler from the pitcher's work.

Our solution to this quandary is Deserved Run Average (DRA), our core pitching metric. DRA looks like earned run average (ERA), the tried-and-true pitching stat you've seen on every baseball broadcast or box score from the past century, but it's very different. To start, DRA takes an event-by-event look at what the pitchers does, and adjusts the value of that event based on different environmental factors like park, batter, catcher, umpire, base-out situation, run differential, inning, defense, home field advantage, pitcher role and temperature. That mixed model gives us a pitcher's expected contribution, similar to what we do for our DRC+ model for hitters and FRAA model for catchers. (Oh, and we also consider the pitcher's effect on basestealing and on balls getting past the catcher.)

It's important to note that DRA is set to the scale of runs allowed per nine innings (RA9) instead of ERA, which makes DRA's scale slightly higher than ERA's. The reason for this is because ERA tends to overrate three types of pitchers:

1. Pitchers who play in parks where scorers hand out more errors. Official scorers differ significantly in the frequency at which they assign errors to fielders.
2. Ground-ball pitchers, because a substantial proportion of errors occur on groundballs.
3. Pitchers who aren't very good. Better pitchers often allow fewer unearned runs than bad pitchers, because good pitchers tend to find ways to get out of jams.

Since the last time you picked up an edition of this book, we've also made a few minor changes to DRA to make it better. Recent research into "tunneling"—the act of throwing consecutive pitches that appear similar from a batter's point of view until after the swing decision point–data has given us a new contextual factor to account for in DRA: plate distance. This refers to the distance between successive pitches as they approach the plate, and while it has a smaller effect than factors like velocity or whiff rate, it still can help explain pitcher strikeout rate in our model.

New Pitching Metrics for 2020

We're including a few "new" pitching metrics in the book for the 2020 edition, though unlike last year, these numbers may be a little bit more familiar to those of you who have spent some time investigating baseball statistics.

Fastball Percentage

Our fastball percentage (FB%) statistic measures how frequently a pitcher throws a pitch classified as a "fastball," measured as a percentage of overall pitches thrown. We qualify three types of fastballs:

1. The traditional four-seam fastball;
2. The two-seam fastball or sinker;
3. "Hard cutters," which are pitches that have the movement profile of a cut fastball and are used as the pitcher's primary offering or in place of a more traditional fastball.

For example, a pitcher with a FB% of 67 throws any combination of these three pitches about two-thirds of the time.

Whiff Rate

Everybody loves a swing and a miss, and whiff rate (WHF) measures how frequently pitchers induce a swinging strike. To calculate WHF, we add up all the pitches thrown that ended with a swinging strike, then divide that number by a pitcher's total pitches thrown. Most often, high whiff rates correlate with high strikeout rates (and overall effective pitcher performance).

Called Strike Probability

Called Strike Probability (CSP) is a number that represents the likelihood that all of a pitcher's pitches will be called a strike while controlling for location, pitcher and batter handedness, umpire and count. Here's how it works: on each pitch, our model determines how many times (out of 100) that a similar pitch was called for a strike given those factors mentioned above, and when normalized for each batter's strike zone. Then we average the CSP for all pitches thrown by a pitcher in a season, and that gives us the yearly CSP percentage you see in the stats boxes.

As you might imagine, pitchers with a higher CSP are more likely to work in the zone, where pitchers with a lower CSP are likely locating their pitches outside the normal strike zone, for better or for worse.

Projections

Many of you aren't turning to this book just for a look at what a player has done, but for a look at what a player is going to do: the PECOTA projections. PECOTA, initially developed by Nate Silver (who has moved on to greater fame as a political analyst), consists of three parts:

1. Major-league equivalencies, which use minor-league statistics to project how a player will perform in the major leagues;
2. Baseline forecasts, which use weighted averages and regression to the mean to estimate a player's current true talent level; and
3. Aging curves, which uses the career paths of comparable players to estimate how a player's statistics are likely to change over time.

With all those important things covered, let's take a look at what's in the book this year.

Team Prospectus

Most of this book is composed of team chapters, with one for each of the 30 major-league franchises. On the first page of each chapter, you'll see a box that contains some of the key statistics for each team as well as a very inviting stadium diagram. (You can see an example of this for the Milwaukee Brewers on this very page!)

We start with the team name, their unadjusted 2019 win-loss record, and their divisional ranking. Beneath that are a host of other team statistics. **Pythag** presents an adjusted 2019 winning percentage, calculated by taking runs scored per game (**RS/G**) and runs allowed per game (**RA/G**) for the team, and running them through a version of Bill James' Pythagorean formula that was refined and improved by David Smyth and Brandon Heipp. (The formula is called "Pythagenpat," which is equally fun to type and to say.)

Next up is **DRC+**, described earlier, to indicate the overall hitting ability of the team either above or below league-average. Run prevention on the pitching side is covered by **DRA** (also mentioned earlier) and another metric: Fielding Independent Pitching (**FIP**), which calculates another ERA-like statistic based on strikeouts, walks, and home runs recorded. Defensive Efficiency Rating (**DER**) tells us the percentage of balls in play turned into outs for the team, and is a quick fielding shorthand that rounds out run prevention.

After that, we have several measures related to roster composition, as opposed to on-field performance. **B-Age** and **P-Age** tell us the average age of a team's batters and pitchers, respectively. **Salary** is the combined team payroll for all on-field players, and Doug Pappas' Marginal Dollars per Marginal Win (**M$/MW**) tells us how much money a team spent to earn production above replacement level.

Ending this batch of statistics is the number of disabled list days a team had over the season (**IL Days**) and the amount of salary paid to players on the disabled list (**$ on IL**); this final number is expressed as a percentage of total payroll.

Next to each of these stats, we've listed each team's MLB rank in that category from first to 30th. In this, first always indicates a positive outcome and 30th a negative outcome, except in the case of salary—first is highest.

After the franchise statistics, we share a few items about the team's home ballpark. There's the aforementioned diagram of the park's dimensions (including distances to the outfield wall), a graphic showing the height of the wall from the left-field pole to the right-field pole, and a table showing three-year park factors for the stadium. The park factors are displayed as indexes where 100 is average, 110 means that the park inflates the statistic in question by 10 percent, and 90 means that the park deflates the statistic in question by 10 percent.

On the second page of each team chapter, you'll find three graphs. The first is the **2019 Hit List Ranking**. This shows our Hit List Rank for the team on each day of the 2019 season and is intended to give you a picture of the ups and downs of the team's season. Hit List Rank measures overall team performance and drives the Hit List Power Rankings at the baseballprospectus.com website.

The second graph is **Committed Payroll** and helps you see how the team's payroll has compared to the MLB and divisional average payrolls over time. Payroll figures are current as of January 1, 2020; with so many free agents still unsigned as of this writing, the final 2020 figure will likely be significantly different for many teams. (In the meantime, you can always find the most current data at Baseball Prospectus' Cot's Baseball Contracts page.)

The third graph is **Farm System Ranking** and displays how the Baseball Prospectus prospect team has ranked the organization's farm system since 2007.

After the graphs, we have a **Personnel** section that lists many of the important decision-makers and upper-level field and operations staff members for the franchise, as well as any former Baseball Prospectus staff members who are currently part of the organization. (In very rare circumstances, someone might be on both lists!)

Juan Soto LF

Born: 10/25/98 Age: 21 Bats: L Throws: L
Height: 6'1" Weight: 185 Origin: International Free Agent, 2015

YEAR	TEAM	LVL	AGE	PA	R	2B	3B	HR	RBI	BB	K	SB	CS	AVG/OBP/SLG
2017	NAT	RK	18	27	3	1	1	0	4	2	1	0	0	.320/.370/.440
2017	HAG	A	18	96	15	5	0	3	14	10	8	1	2	.360/.427/.523
2018	HAG	A	19	74	12	5	3	5	24	14	13	2	0	.373/.486/.814
2018	POT	A+	19	73	17	3	1	7	18	11	8	0	1	.371/.466/.790
2018	HAR	AA	19	35	4	2	0	2	10	4	7	1	0	.323/.400/.581
2018	WAS	MLB	19	494	77	25	1	22	70	79	99	5	2	.292/.406/.517
2019	WAS	MLB	20	659	110	32	5	34	110	108	132	12	1	.282/.401/.548
2020	WAS	MLB	21	630	92	30	3	35	102	85	123	5	2	.284/.382/.543

Comparables: Ronald Acuña Jr., Mike Trout, Tony Conigliaro

YEAR	TEAM	LVL	AGE	PA	DRC+	VORP	BABIP	BRR	FRAA	WARP
2017	NAT	RK	18	27	135	1.5	.333	0.0	RF(9): -1.1	0.0
2017	HAG	A	18	96	181	8.0	.373	1.0	RF(19): -1.9, LF(2): -0.3	0.9
2018	HAG	A	19	74	222	14.5	.405	0.3	RF(14): 1.1, CF(2): 0.2	1.2
2018	POT	A+	19	73	260	15.4	.340	1.4	RF(14): 1.0, LF(1): 0.0	1.6
2018	HAR	AA	19	35	113	3.6	.364	0.0	LF(4): 0.6, RF(4): -0.5	0.1
2018	WAS	MLB	19	494	125	40.5	.338	-0.5	LF(114): 2.7	3.0
2019	WAS	MLB	20	659	136	49.0	.312	1.4	LF(150): -0.8	4.9
2020	WAS	MLB	21	630	133	43.6	.310	-0.1	LF 3	4.8

Position Players

After all that information and a thoughtful bylined essay covering each team, we present our player comments. These are also bylined, but due to frequent franchise shifts during the offseason, our bylines are more a rough guide than a perfect accounting of who wrote what.

Each player is listed with the major-league team that employed him as of early January 2020. If a player changed teams after that point via free agency, trade, or any other method, you'll be able to find them in the chapter for their previous squad.

As an example, take a look at the player comment for Nationals outfielder Juan Soto: the stat block that accompanies his written comment is at the top of this page. First we cover biographical information (age is as of June 30, 2020) before moving onto the stats themselves. Our statistic columns include standard identifying information like **YEAR**, **TEAM**, **LVL** (level of affiliated play) and **AGE** before getting into the numbers. Next, we provide raw, untranslated numbers like you might find on the back of your dad's baseball cards: **PA** (plate appearances), **R** (runs), **2B** (doubles), **3B** (triples), **HR** (home runs), **RBI** (runs batted in), **BB** (walks), **K** (strikeouts), **SB** (stolen bases) and **CS** (caught stealing).

Next, we have unadjusted "slash" statistics: **AVG** (batting average), **OBP** (on-base percentage) and **SLG** (slugging percentage). Following the slash line is **DRC+** (Deserved Runs Created Plus), which we described earlier as total offensive expected contribution compared to the league average.

One of our oldest active metrics, **VORP** (Value Over Replacement Player), considers offensive production, position and plate appearances. In essence, it is the number of runs contributed beyond what a replacement-level player at the same position would contribute if given the same percentage of team plate appearances. VORP does not consider the quality of a player's defense.

BABIP (batting average on balls in play) tells us how often a ball in play fell for a hit, and can help us identify whether a batter may have been lucky or not...but note that high BABIPs also tend to follow the great hitters of our time, as well as speedy singles hitters who put the ball on the ground.

The next item is **BRR** (Baserunning Runs), which covers all of a player's baserunning accomplishments including (but not limited to) swiped bags and failed attempts. Next is **FRAA** (Fielding Runs Above Average), which also includes the number of games previously played at each position noted in parentheses. Multi-position players have only their two most frequent positions listed here, but their total FRAA number reflects all positions played.

Our last column here is **WARP** (Wins Above Replacement Player). WARP estimates the total value of a player, which means for hitters it takes into account hitting runs above average (calculated using the DRC+ model), BRR and FRAA. Then, it makes an adjustment for positions played and gives the player a credit for plate appearances based upon the difference between "replacement level"—which is derived from the quality of players added to a team's roster after the start of the season—and the league average.

The final line just below the stats box is **PECOTA** data, which is discussed further in a following section.

Catchers

Catchers are a special breed, and thus they have earned their own separate box which displays some of the defensive metrics that we've built just for them. As an example, let's check out J.T. Realmuto.

The **YEAR** and **TEAM** columns match what you'd find in the other stat box. **P. COUNT** indicates the number of pitches thrown while the catcher was behind the plate, including swinging strikes, fouls and balls in play. **FRM RUNS** is the total run value the catcher provided (or cost) his team by influencing the umpire to call strikes where other catchers did not. **BLK RUNS** expresses the total run value above or below average for the catcher's ability to prevent wild pitches and passed balls. **THRW RUNS** is calculated using a similar model as the previous two statistics, and it measures a catcher's ability to throw out basestealers but also to dissuade them from testing his arm in the first place. It takes into account factors like the pitcher (including his delivery and pickoff move) and baserunner (who could be as fast as Billy Hamilton or as slow as Yonder Alonso). **TOT RUNS** is the sum of all of the previous three statistics.

Justin Verlander   RHP
Born: 02/20/83   Age: 37   Bats: R   Throws: R
Height: 6'5"   Weight: 225   Origin: Round 1, 2004 Draft (#2 overall)

YEAR	TEAM	LVL	AGE	W	L	SV	G	GS	IP	H	HR	BB/9	K/9	K	GB%	BABIP
2017	DET	MLB	34	10	8	0	28	28	172	153	23	3.5	9.2	176	34%	.283
2017	HOU	MLB	34	5	0	0	5	5	34	17	4	1.3	11.4	43	32%	.194
2018	HOU	MLB	35	16	9	0	34	34	214	156	28	1.6	12.2	290	31%	.272
2019	HOU	MLB	36	21	6	0	34	34	223	137	36	1.7	12.1	300	36%	.219
2020	HOU	MLB	37	15	6	0	29	29	184	138	28	2.3	12.1	248	35%	.274

Comparables: Zack Greinke, A.J. Burnett, Aníbal Sánchez

YEAR	TEAM	LVL	AGE	WHIP	ERA	DRA	WARP	MPH	FB%	WHF	CSP
2017	DET	MLB	34	1.28	3.82	4.03	3.0	97.7	58	11	47.8
2017	HOU	MLB	34	0.65	1.06	3.08	0.9	97.5	59.6	15.1	49.9
2018	HOU	MLB	35	0.90	2.52	2.33	7.3	97.5	61.2	16.2	51.6
2019	HOU	MLB	36	0.80	2.58	2.51	7.9	96.8	49.9	17.5	48.3
2020	HOU	MLB	37	1.01	2.75	2.95	5.3	95.8	54.6	15.1	48.2

Pitchers

Let's give our pitchers a turn, using 2019 AL Cy Young winner Justin Verlander as our example. Take a look at his stat block: the first line and the **YEAR**, **TEAM**, **LVL** and **AGE** columns are the same as in the position player example earlier.

Here too, we have a series of columns that display raw, unadjusted statistics compiled by the pitcher over the course of a season: **W** (wins), **L** (losses), **SV** (saves), **G** (games pitched), **GS** (games started), **IP** (innings pitched), **H** (hits allowed) and **HR** (home runs allowed). Next we have two statistics that are rates: **BB/9** (walks per nine innings) and **K/9** (strikeouts per nine innings), before returning to the unadjusted K (strikeouts).

Next up is **GB%** (ground ball percentage), which is the percentage of all batted balls that were hit on the ground, including both outs and hits. Remember, this is based on observational data and subject to human error, so please approach this with a healthy dose of skepticism.

BABIP (batting average on balls in play) is calculated using the same methodology as it is for position players, but it often tells us more about a pitcher than it does a hitter. With pitchers, a high BABIP is often due to poor defense or bad luck, and can often be an indicator of potential rebound, and a low BABIP may be cause to expect performance regression. (A typical league-average BABIP is close to .290-.300.)

Cincinnati Reds 2020

The metrics **WHIP** (walks plus hits per inning pitched) and **ERA** (earned run average) are old standbys: WHIP measures walks and hits allowed on a per-inning basis, while ERA measures earned runs on a nine-inning basis. Neither of these stats are translated or adjusted.

DRA (Deserved Run Average) was described at length earlier, and measures how many runs the pitcher "deserved" to allow per nine innings. Please note that since we lack all the data points that would make for a "real" DRA for minor-league events, the DRA displayed for minor league partial-seasons is based off of different data. (That data is a modified version of our cFIP metric, which you can find more information about on our website.)

Just like with hitters, **WARP** (Wins Above Replacement Player) is a total value metric that puts pitchers of all stripes on the same scale as position players. We use DRA as the primary input for our calculation of WARP. You might notice that relief pitchers (due to their limited innings) may have a lower WARP than you were expecting or than you might see in other WARP-like metrics. WARP does not take leverage into account, just the actions a pitcher performs and the expected value of those actions...which ends up judging high-leverage relief pitchers differently than you might imagine given their prestige and market value.

MPH gives you the pitcher's 95th percentile velocity for the noted season, in order to give you an idea of what the *peak* fastball velocity a pitcher possesses. Since this comes from our pitch-tracking data, it is not publicly available for minor-league pitchers.

Finally, we display the three new pitching metrics we described earlier. **FB%** (fastball percentage) gives you the percentage of fastballs thrown out of all pitches. **WHF** (whiff rate) tells you the percentage of swinging strikes induced out of all pitches. **CSP** (called strike probability) expresses the likelihood of all pitches thrown to result in a called strike, after controlling for factors like handedness, umpire, pitch type, count and location.

PECOTA

All players have PECOTA projections for 2020, as well as a set of other numbers that describe the performance of comparable players according to PECOTA. All projections for 2020 are for the player at the date we went to press in early January and are projected into the league and park context as indicated by the team abbreviation. (Note that players at very low levels of the minors are too unpredictable to assess using these numbers.) All PECOTA projected statistics represent a player's projected major-league performance.

Below the projections are the player's three highest-scoring comparable players as determined by PECOTA. All comparables represent a snapshot of how the listed player was performing at the same age as the current player, so if a

23-year-old pitcher is compared to Bartolo Colón, he's actually being compared to a 23-year-old Colón, not the version that pitched for the Rangers in 2018, nor to Colón's career as a whole.

A few points about pitcher projections. First, we aren't yet projecting peak velocity, so that column will be blank in the PECOTA lines. Second, projecting DRA is trickier than evaluating past performance, because it is unclear how deserving each pitcher will be of his anticipated outcomes. However, we know that another DRA-related statistic–contextual FIP or cFIP-estimates future run scoring very well. So for PECOTA, the projected DRA figures you see are based on the past cFIPs generated by the pitcher and comparable players over time, along with the other factors described above.

Lineouts

In each chapter's Lineouts section, you'll find abbreviated text comments, as well as all the same information you'd find in our full player comments. The only difference is that we limit the stats boxes in this section to only including the 2019 information for each player.

Managers

After all those wonderful team chapters, we've got statistics for each big-league manager, all of whom are organized by alphabetical order. Here you'll find a block including an extraordinary amount of information collected from each manager's entire career. For more information on the acronyms and what they mean, please visit the Glossary at www.baseballprospectus.com.

There is one important metric that we'd like to call attention to, and you'll find it next to each manager's name: **wRM+** (weighted reliever management plus). Developed by Rob Arthur and Rian Watt, wRM+ investigates how good a manager is at using their best relievers during the moments of highest leverage, using both our proprietary DRA metric as well as Leverage Index. wRM+ is scaled to a league average of 100, and a wRM+ of 105 indicates that relievers were used approximately five percent "better" than average. On the other hand, a wRM+ of 95 would tell us the team used its relievers five percent "worse" than the average team.

While wRM+ does not have an extremely strong correlation with a manager, it is statistically significant; this means that a manager is not *entirely* responsible for a team's wRM+, but does have some effect on that number.

PECOTA Leaderboards

If you're familiar with PECOTA, then you'll have noticed that the projection system often appears bullish on players coming off a bad year and bearish on players coming off a good year. (This is because the system weights several previous seasons, not just the most recent one.) In addition, we publish the 50th

Cincinnati Reds 2020

percentile projections for each player–which is smack in the middle of the range of projected production—which tends to mean PECOTA stat lines don't often have extreme results like 40 home runs or 250 strikeouts in a given season. In essence, PECOTA doesn't project very many extreme seasons.

At the end of the book, we've ranked the top players at each position based on their PECOTA projections. This might help you visualize just how a given player's projection compares to that of their peers, so that even if a dramatic stat line isn't projected, you can still imagine how they stack up against the rest of the league.

xvi - Statistical Introduction

Part 1: Team Analysis

Cincinnati Reds: Where Are You Going, Where Have You Been?

Zach Crizer, Keanan Lamb and Matthew Trueblood

2019: What Went Right

The roles baseball teams play in the lives of their fans has never totally aligned with their goals on the field. Winning inspires a great deal of satisfaction, yes, but everyone realizes the thrills of late October aren't enough to support the other six or seven-and-a-half months of daily attention. No, the point of baseball teams is to provide something interesting for every day of halfway seasonable weather that the year has to offer. In short, simply to be worthy of the stage. In this way the 2019 Reds fulfilled their mission with aplomb.

This manifested most memorably in a brawl for the ages, a real live two-way player, a 49-homer season and a couple star turns in the rotation, but it started with a winter of trying. Under the leadership of Dick Williams, the Reds looked at a .500ish team and decided to supplement it with established-if-volatile veteran players who might help them contend for a wild card—a rare traveling of the middle road. They saved one-time ace Sonny Gray from a nightmarish stint with the Yankees, plugged the steady Tanner Roark into what had long been a black hole of a rotation, and took a flier on Yasiel Puig in a contract year.

They also lured pitching coach Derek Johnson away from the Brewers and hitting coach Turner Ward from the Dodgers. As hard as coaches are to evaluate, Johnson (don't know if you heard, but he worked with Gray in college!) rates as a brilliant hire. Like a restored muscle car, Gray was better than ever. With a 2.87 ERA and 61 DRA-, he's having the best season of his career by just about any metric you can find, enjoying more comfort with a repertoire that has always been enigmatic.

By BP's metrics, the Reds had two of the 20 most valuable pitchers in baseball last year. The other, of course, was Luis Castillo. After a stellar half-season debut in 2017 and a rougher sophomore campaign in 2018, the Pedro Martinez-esque 26-year-old amplified his world-beating changeup at Johnson's behest. Sticking diligently to a barrel-missing plan and sometimes totally overpowering opponents—he had three of the majors' 28 individual pitching performances with 25+ whiffs—Castillo ranks as one of the dozen best starters in the game. It's hard to come up with good reasons why he can't maintain that status going forward.

Gray and Castillo's leaps forward are the most calculus-changing positives from 2019, but the rest of the roster was also commendable for that all-important entertainment factor. Reliever Michael Lorenzen actually became *two-way player* Michael Lorenzen. Aristides Aquino is probably not an all-around star going forward, but the man can hit some dingers. Eugenio Suárez, signed to a long-term deal, didn't necessarily produce more than he did in a terrific 2018 (his 132 DRC+ is functionally the same as last season's 136), but virtually matching it in the form of 49 homers (and racing Pete Alonso for black ink) was undeniably more thrilling.

Finally, Amir Garrett charged the Pirates dugout. Shortly after news broke that Puig had been traded, the Reds reliever did what many baseball folks felt like doing and sparked a series of events that made Cincinnati the setting for the season's best GET TO ANY DEVICE THAT PLAYS VIDEO moment. Cincinnati! While we don't condone the actual fighting, people will still be talking about the brawl for years, and probably about some of the other attention-demanding things the 2019 Reds did as well. None of it happened by accident, and it's worth applauding.

2019: What Went Wrong

On the most basic level, the Reds vastly underperformed their run differential, especially early in the season. A team that outscored its opponents for most of the season (they finished just underwater at 701-711) finished more than 10 games under .500 and lost touch with any hope of serious contention in the heat of the summer. The Reds hit .236/.307/.390 in high-leverage situations, one of the worst marks in the league. That is to say that with close games hanging in the balance, they hit like Leury García. This brings up an uncomfortable conversation: Shortstop José Iglesias wound up as the Reds' second-most productive position player behind Suárez. This is a little bit of a lie for effect. Iglesias had the team's second-highest WARP, but he gained much of it on defense. He's only a smidge ahead of solid catcher Tucker Barnhart (who missed some time with injury) and Jesse Winker, who has been the second-most consistent offensive force.

Force is sort of a misnomer for most Reds hitters outside of Suárez and Aquino, unfortunately. Winker had a 115 DRC+, but his excellent plate judgment has not translated to significant power. Nick Senzel's injury-curtailed debut left something to be desired; despite polish and well-roundedness being the selling points, more on-base ability is going to be expected in the future. For others, like José Peraza, the days of "expecting more" down the line have given way to the desperate reality of an untenable .631 OPS. He was subsequently non-tendered. Joey Votto, meanwhile, has finally reached a stage of undeniable decline as he turns 36. He's still getting on base at a .359 clip, but a total power outage has made for a pedestrian performance. Waiting for Votto to turn on the jets, only to watch as he labored on, was a most crushing dose of reality on an otherwise fun Reds club. —*Zach Crizer*

Prospect Outlook

Few organizations have seen the kind of turnover in their system in a single year than the Reds. Whether it be graduating to the big leagues (Nick Senzel), traded (Taylor Trammell, Shed Long, Josiah Gray, Jeter Downs), or lost to injury (Hunter Greene) it was a tumultuous year down on the farm. In addition to the tumult, other top prospects struggled during the 2019 season and their future contributions to the parent club are in question.

Jonathan India, the Reds' first rounder of 2018, was pushed to Double-A Chattanooga despite pedestrian numbers in the Florida State League. However, he showed signs of an improved approach in the final month, with an abbreviated swing that produced better power and walk numbers. Righty pitcher **Tony Santillan** could not replicate his breakout 2018 campaign with reduced command—his BB/9 doubled from 2.3 to 4.7. Both India and Santillan are closest to the majors but require extra seasoning before promotion.

Two names to watch are catcher **Tyler Stephenson** and shortstop **Jose Israel Garcia**. Both participated in the Arizona Fall League after strong finishes to their regular seasons. Stephenson hasn't quite found the power stroke many envisioned the 6-foot-4 backstop would feature coming out of high school but has turned into a capable defender despite his larger frame—slashing .285/.372/.410 in the Southern League is no small feat. Garcia got off to a slow start but finished admirably while showcasing good athletic ability from short. —*Keanan Lamb*

2020 Outlook

In the minds of top Reds executives Dick Williams and Nick Krall, 2020 began at the trade deadline. If that hadn't been their mentality, they surely wouldn't have chosen Trevor Bauer as their target when shopping Puig. However, because getting Bauer also cost the team Taylor Trammell, the team faced immediate pressure (specifically) to shore up their outfield and (broadly) assemble a roster that justifies really going for it. With fearlessness and creativity, they managed it.

It's just barely fair to call the four-year, $64-million contracts to which Cincinnati signed Mike Moustakas and Nick Castellanos twin pacts. In reality, Moustakas's deal (which came very early in free agency and announced the Reds as serious shoppers) isn't nearly as rich as Castellanos's, because despite the deferrals in the Castellanos contract, there are two opt-outs and a mutual option with a buyout attached for 2024. Both are risky moves. Moustakas has been a consistent and underrated hitter, with a broader base of skills than he gets credit for, but he's also a 31-year-old trying to move up the defensive spectrum to second base. Castellanos is young and has been brilliant recently, but his defense has been an adventure at every position he's tried, and his unorthodox mechanics and approach make him hard to project. There's a nightmare scenario in which the team is saddled with two unproductive players at handsome salaries, and Castellanos's opt-outs put a ceiling on the upside of the transaction bundle.

Shogo Akiyama presents a very different kind of risk. He's been a steady producer in Japan and passes the eye test as a defensive center fielder, especially in the small center fields of the NL Central. He also comes cheaply compared to Moustakas and Castellanos, and there seems to be considerably more upside in his contract. On the other hand, it's still hard to reliably predict the way production will translate when players switch continents, and Akiyama is even older than Moustakas. Add the entire trio to Eugenio Suárez and Joey Votto, and it's a surprisingly expensive and middle-aged positional core. Still, it's a good one, and only the worst quartile of possible outcomes would really render it otherwise.

The team's pitching infrastructure is much less centered on individuals and much more systematic. Coach Johnson was as much of a breakout star as Gray or Castillo last year. With those two and Bauer in the mix, the team didn't feel tremendous pressure to make a big splash with a free-agent hurler. They were in on Zack Wheeler, but let the Phillies pay for his measurables and upside. Instead, they elected to bet on Wade Miley's lower-wattage consistency. Johnson and Miley were together with the 2018 Brewers, when Miley first really found the cutter that has rejuvenated him, so the fit is perfect. By adding Pedro Strop to a deep but star-starved bullpen, the team put a solid finishing touch on the rapid creation of a contender, albeit one without the youth and dynamism of so many recent rebuilders. Then again, that just means that they more closely mirror the defending World Series champions than any of the teams they beat in October.
—Matthew Trueblood

Performance Graphs

2019 Hit List Ranking

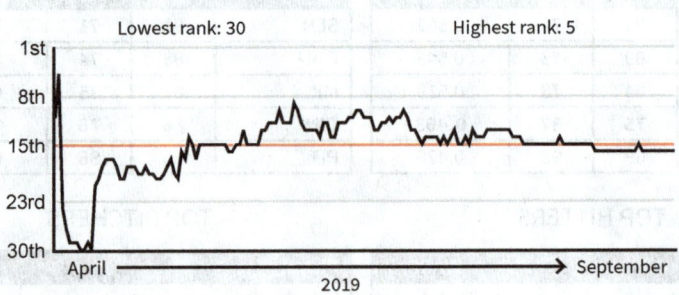

Committed Payroll (in millions)

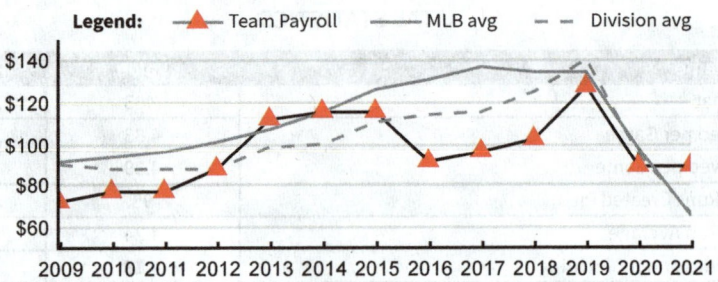

Farm System Ranking

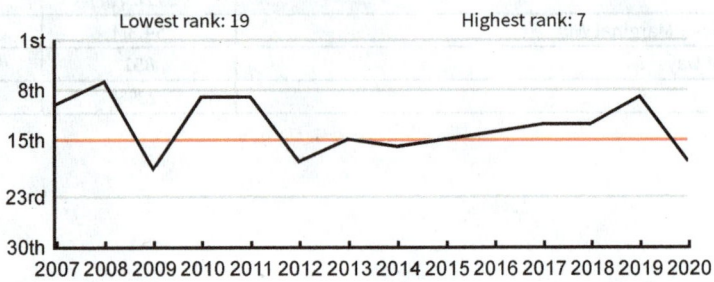

2019 Team Performance

ACTUAL STANDINGS

Team	W	L	Pct
SLN	91	71	0.562
MIL	89	73	0.549
CHN	84	78	0.519
CIN	**75**	**87**	**0.463**
PIT	69	93	0.426

THIRD-ORDER STANDINGS

Team	W	L	Pct
SLN	91	71	0.564
CHN	88	74	0.543
MIL	87	75	0.535
CIN	**86**	**76**	**0.534**
PIT	66	96	0.407

TOP HITTERS

Player	WARP
Eugenio Suárez	4.4
José Iglesias	2.5
Tucker Barnhart	2.5

TOP PITCHERS

Player	WARP
Luis Castillo	5.7
Sonny Gray	5.3
Anthony DeSclafani	3.3

VITAL STATISTICS

Statistic Name	Value	Rank
Pythagenpat	.493	16th
Runs Scored per Game	4.33	25th
Runs Allowed per Game	4.39	7th
Deserved Runs Created Plus	93	20th
Deserved Run Average	4.24	7th
Fielding Independent Pitching	4.18	9th
Defensive Efficiency Rating	.714	6th
Batter Age	27.8	12th
Pitcher Age	28.1	16th
Salary	$126.7M	15th
Marginal $ per Marginal Win	$4.3M	12th
Injured List Days	851	6th
$ on IL	23%	24th

2020 Team Projections

PROJECTED STANDINGS

Team	W	L	Pct	+/-
CIN	86.1	75.9	0.531	11
CHN	84.5	77.5	0.522	0
SLN	80.3	81.7	0.496	-11
MIL	79.4	82.6	0.490	-10
PIT	70.3	91.7	0.434	1

TOP PROJECTED HITTERS

Player	WARP
Eugenio Suárez	3.0
Shogo Akiyama	2.9
Joey Votto	2.7

TOP PROJECTED PITCHERS

Player	WARP
Luis Castillo	3.6
Sonny Gray	3.2
Trevor Bauer	2.9

FARM SYSTEM REPORT

Top Prospect	Number of Top 101 Prospects
Nick Lodolo, #59	1

KEY DEDUCTIONS

Player	WARP
José Iglesias	1.2
Kevin Gausman	1.1
Alex Wood	0.9
José Peraza	0.4
Jose Siri	0.1
Brian O'Grady	0.0
Jimmy Herget	-1.1

KEY ADDITIONS

Player	WARP
Shogo Akiyama	2.9
Nicholas Castellanos	2.3
Mike Moustakas	2.0
Mark Payton	1.2
Wade Miley	0.7
Pedro Strop	0.7
Nate Jones	0.3
Travis Jankowski	0.1
José De León	0.1
Ryan Hendrix	0.1

Team Personnel

President of Baseball Operations
Dick Williams

Vice President & General Manager
Nick Krall

Vice President, Assistant General Manager
Sam Grossman

Vice President, Player Personnel
Chris Buckley

Manager
David Bell

BP Alumni
Stuart Wallace

Great American Ball Park Stats

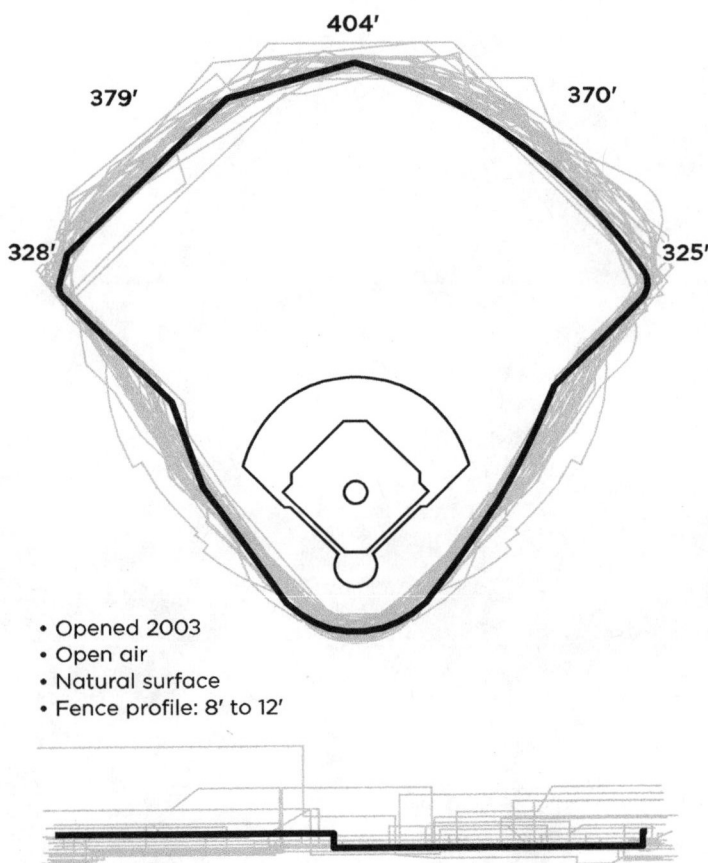

- Opened 2003
- Open air
- Natural surface
- Fence profile: 8' to 12'

Three-Year Park Factors

Runs	Runs/RH	Runs/LH	HR/RH	HR/LH
102	101	104	110	109

Great American Ball Park Stats

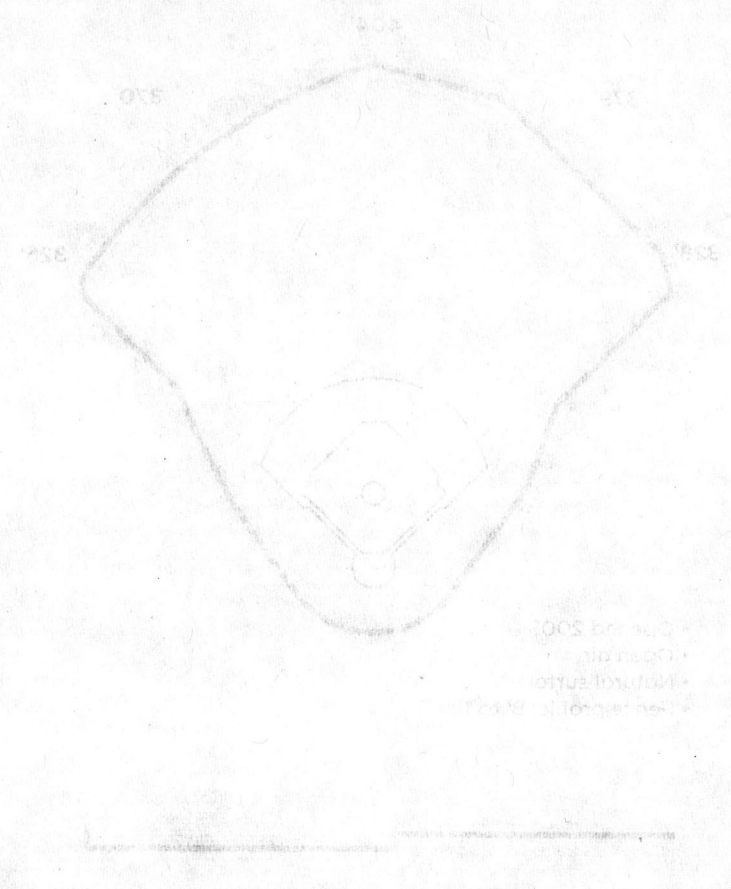

Reds Team Analysis

When spring training commenced last year, it marked the first time since the Dusty Baker era that the Cincinnati Reds stretched and played long toss in an optimistic air. The Reds' front office, led by Dick Williams and Nick Krall, had spent the winter completing a series of deals that signaled a "win-now" mentality. There was Tanner Roark, and Yasiel Puig, and Matt Kemp, and Alex Wood and Sonny Gray. (Jose Iglesias and Derek Dietrich were also added, and played larger-than-expected roles.) In an era of constant fretting over the luxury tax, club control and financial flexibility, the Reds emerged as the iconoclast—the team who wanted to win, even if it meant spending more money and punting away potential league-minimum labor.

The Reds' investment in their on-the-field product was rewarded in a sense—attendance improved for the first time in years—and not in another. Improving by 10 wins, to a 75-87 mark, was enough to net them fourth place. It was not enough to end their playoff drought (now the sixth longest in the majors) or their streak of consecutive losing seasons (six and counting). Some teams would have hit the reset button and conformed in response, thinking to themselves, "Ah, well, that didn't work." The Reds, though, doubled down.

The most obvious sign of this was Cincinnati's continued willingness to do deals others would bristle at as inefficient. Hence Krall's decision to sign infielder Mike Moustakas to a four-year deal worth $64 million, and left-hander Wade Miley to a two-year pact worth $15 million. Neither seemed like the cleanest fit on a roster that already had a third baseman (and required its top infield prospect to move to the outfield a year ago) and a loaded rotation. Yet both could pay off.

Last season, Cincinnati's various second basemen combined to hit .221/.288/.390 with 23 home runs. Moustakas, comparatively, has averaged 34 home runs over the past three years. The Reds were tied for 18th in the majors in DRC+, a mark that placed them in the same ballpark as bottom feeders like the Toronto Blue Jays, Colorado Rockies, Kansas City Royals and Pittsburgh Pirates. They needed the offensive help, in other words, and that should make Moustakas a welcomed addition—at least offensively.

Miley seemed well on his way to a richer multi-year deal before the All-Star Game. He entered the Midsummer Classic with a 3.28 ERA and 2.61 strikeout-to-walk ratio in 18 starts. The second half was considerably less kind to Miley, however, and he ended the year with an atrocious September—and we mean atrocious. Miley yielded 28 hits and 21 runs in 11 innings across five starts. The Reds can only hope Miley experiences a bounce-back season now that he's reunited with an old pitching coach.

The more interesting aspect of the Reds' winter was how they went all-in on eschewing pitching tradition. The transformation started last offseason when the team hired well-respected pitching coach Derek Johnson from the Milwaukee Brewers. Unlike with their win-now trades, the Reds saw nothing but positive results from Johnson's hiring.

Johnson's mystique dated back to his time at Vanderbilt University, where he coached from 2002 to 2012 and worked with countless future professionals, including David Price, Mike Minor and Gray. For as often as he brushed shoulders with blue chippers while overseeing the Commodores, he proved his touch was as effective with the at-times ragtag Brewers' staffs.

Under Johnson's instruction, Brewers pitchers had exceeded expectations in each of the past two seasons, even coming within a win of the 2018 World Series. There were countless anecdotes about how Johnson massaged the Brewers' unique staff—devoid of a front-line starter and often resorted to bullpen games in the postseason—to success. Some choice cuts included him helping Miley command a new cutter; aiding Jhoulys Chacin with the hunt for a changeup grip; and assisting Corbin Burnes adapt to a new role. No matter who and no matter what, Johnson always seems to have the ability to connect and correct.

"I don't think he has a secret potion of a formula or like, everyone's glove side is doing this or everyone's arm action has to do this," Gray told The Athletic last season. "It's everyone. I mean, he obviously teaches those things, but he teaches guys about themselves and what they need to do...he lets guys kind of be themselves, and helps them be the best version of themselves."

The numbers validate Gray's assertion. In Johnson's first year at the helm, Reds starters pitched to a runs-per-nine rate of 4.39, the ninth-best in baseball and a stark improvement over their previous mark (5.45, which ranked 26th). We can, of course, go deeper than that. The Reds' 4.05 rotational DRA was sixth in baseball, behind a quintet of teams with much better records: the Los Angeles Dodgers, Washington Nationals, New York Mets, Houston Astros, and Tampa Bay Rays. Their 1.39-run improvement in DRA was the largest in the sport.

But, while Gray said there's no set formula, it seemed like Johnson did instill in the Reds a predilection for the high fastball.

Throwing high fastballs is a tactic that has grown in popularity for obvious reasons: high heaters are harder to make contact with, leading to more whiffs and more weak contact. The league as a whole last season threw 40.4 percent of its four-seam fastballs in the upper-third of the strike zone or higher. (For reference, in 2018 that percentage was 37.8.) Johnson's pitching philosophy helped contribute to the trend. Don't believe us? Take a look at the table below, which shows team-wide rates for four-seam fastballs thrown in the upper third of the strike zone (or higher) since 2008. The 2019 Reds, as well as three other teams from last year, are in the top 10:

Rank	Team	High Fastball Rate
1	2019 Red Sox	52.7%
2	2017 Red Sox	51.8%
3	2018 Red Sox	51.7%
4	2019 Rays	48.5%
5	2016 Rays	47.0%
6	2016 Red Sox	46.3%
7	2019 Reds	45.7%
8	2019 Marlins	45.4%
9	2016 Tigers	45.4%
1	2014 Nationals	44.9%

The Boston Red Sox, with a similar overhaul of their pitching strategy in the latter half of the decade, have been in a league of their own with only the Rays posing a threat. The Reds weren't too far off, though, at seventh out of the 360 individual team seasons since 2008.

To be clear, this wasn't a case where the Reds were already into high fastballs before Johnson took over the reins, either. Going back as far as we have pitch tracking data, the only increase larger than the Reds' last year (just shy of 12 percent) was actually from another 2019 team: the Marlins, at 13.1 percentage points. Predictably, a number of mainstay Reds pitchers saw large jumps in their high fastball rate from the previous year: Anthony DeSclafani (20 percentage points), Michael Lorenzen (18) and Luis Castillo (16) included. (Even Gray, Johnson's former pupil in college, had his go up by 10 percentage points.) In turn, the fastball whiffs-per-swing rates for DeSclafani, Lorenzen and Castillo were all substantially higher last year than in 2018—in other words, the strategy had a direct benefit for those who bought in.

Keep in mind, that's just one detectable philosophical shift imparted by Johnson during his season in town—one that suggests, of course, that his hiring has already been a fruitful one. Perhaps those results emboldened the Reds to go all-in on a new approach this winter, as they altered their organizational pitching philosophy in an unprecedented way.

Former big-league pitcher and Johnson study Caleb Cotham, who had served as the team's assistant pitching coach for a year, was given a new title right after the season ended: director of pitching. The Reds also hired Kyle Boddy, founder of the Driveline Baseball facility, as their director of pitching initiatives and pitching coordinator. Boddy was brought on to help provide what he described as a "unified decision-making model from top to bottom." Accordingly, the Reds then hired countless coaches and instructors with Driveline ties.

Cincinnati Reds 2020

Clearly the Reds are heavily invested in creating a pitching development pipeline informed by the latest methods and techniques. Whether or not it pays off is to be seen. But there's something to be said about committing to a vision. These days the view of teams is the same as airplane seats: the worst spot is in the middle. That can apply to strategies, too. The Reds could have continued to operate like every other franchise. But it's more interesting (and potentially rewarding, for all we know at this point) that they've deviated from the norm in a significant way.

On paper, the Reds don't match up with the favorites of the division. Their roster has its pluses: Eugenio Suárez is a hidden gem; Nick Senzel could win a batting title someday; we're not quite ready to write off Joey Votto; and so on. But this is a group that needs to be aggressive and to approach things from a different vantage point in order to succeed. Based on the last two offseasons, it seems like the Reds are willing to do both.

Now, it's time for the record to match the boldness.

—*Lucas Apostoleris is an author of Baseball Prospectus.*

Part 2: Player Analysis

PLAYER COMMENTS WITH GRAPHS

Aristides Aquino   RF
Born: 04/22/94   Age: 26   Bats: R   Throws: R
Height: 6'4"   Weight: 220   Origin: International Free Agent, 2011

YEAR	TEAM	LVL	AGE	PA	R	2B	3B	HR	RBI	BB	K	SB	CS	AVG/OBP/SLG
2017	PEN	AA	23	504	54	20	6	17	56	39	145	9	3	.216/.282/.397
2018	PEN	AA	24	445	49	20	2	20	55	35	112	4	5	.240/.306/.448
2018	CIN	MLB	24	1	0	0	0	0	0	0	1	0	0	.000/.000/.000
2019	LOU	AAA	25	323	56	13	1	28	53	23	81	5	1	.299/.356/.636
2019	CIN	MLB	25	225	31	8	0	19	47	16	60	7	0	.259/.316/.576
2020	CIN	MLB	26	462	68	19	2	35	86	28	.134	4	2	.255/.308/.555

Comparables: Lane Adams, Aaron Altherr, Kennys Vargas

Aquino is an extreme example of how modern player development can frustrate prospect evaluation. He produced just middling results after two tries in Double-A, with power appearing to be his only plus tool. Accordingly, we had him outside of the Reds' top 10 list coming into 2019 (although he did get an honorable mention). After a swing change, Aquino laid waste to Triple-A and didn't look back, hitting 11 home runs in his first 16 major-league games following an August call-up. It was a dramatic showing, and one that all but forced us to recalibrate our expectations for him moving forward. Still, we feel it's worth noting that he slowed down from his initial historic run (how could he not?), and that his profile remains that of a high-strikeout/low-walk slugger who's a little older than you'd think. There's volatility in them there mountains, in other words, even if the peaks are taller than we originally estimated.

YEAR	TEAM	LVL	AGE	PA	DRC+	VORP	BABIP	BRR	FRAA	WARP
2017	PEN	AA	23	504	73	-2.2	.274	-0.9	RF(128): 8.9	0.7
2018	PEN	AA	24	445	103	8.2	.282	-1.3	RF(108): 7.7	1.7
2018	CIN	MLB	24	1	87	-0.9	--	-0.7	RF(1): -0.1	-0.1
2019	LOU	AAA	25	323	149	22.7	.321	0.2	RF(64): 3.4, CF(5): 1.8	2.9
2019	CIN	MLB	25	225	114	9.5	.266	0.3	RF(54): 0.9	1.0
2020	CIN	MLB	26	462	118	19.5	.285	-1.3	RF 3	2.3

Aristides Aquino, continued

Batted Ball Distribution

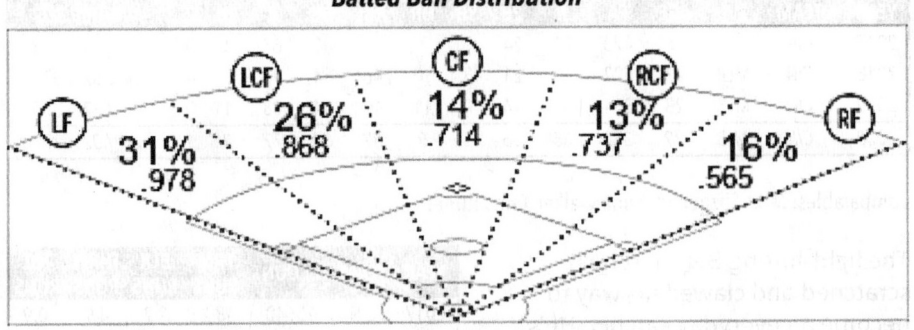

Strike Zone vs LHP   **Strike Zone vs RHP**

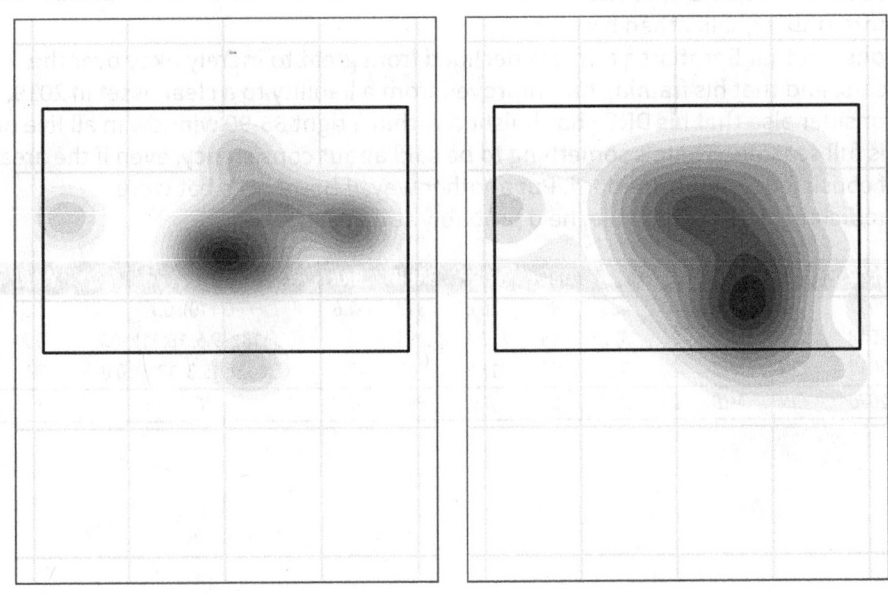

Cincinnati Reds 2020

Tucker Barnhart C
Born: 01/07/91 Age: 29 Bats: L Throws: R
Height: 5'11" Weight: 192 Origin: Round 10, 2009 Draft (#299 overall)

YEAR	TEAM	LVL	AGE	PA	R	2B	3B	HR	RBI	BB	K	SB	CS	AVG/OBP/SLG
2017	CIN	MLB	26	423	26	24	2	7	44	42	68	4	0	.270/.347/.403
2018	CIN	MLB	27	522	50	21	3	10	46	54	96	0	4	.248/.328/.372
2019	CIN	MLB	28	364	32	14	0	11	40	44	83	1	0	.231/.328/.380
2020	CIN	MLB	29	350	36	16	1	9	37	37	77	2	1	.241/.325/.379

Comparables: Mike Fitzgerald, Rube Walker, Chris Turner

The light-hitting Barnhart has scratched and clawed his way to become an everyday catcher. He's done that despite an odd twist that has seen his bat—again, the weaker aspect of his game—prove to be a more stable quality than his mitt.

YEAR	TEAM	P. COUNT	FRM RUNS	BLK RUNS	THRW RUNS	TOT RUNS
2017	CIN	15640	-8.2	2.7	4.9	-0.9
2018	CIN	16826	-11.5	3.6	-0.3	-8.4
2019	CIN	12997	10.1	4.9	-0.3	14.7
2020	CIN	16840	-0.3	2.3	-0.2	1.8

Consider that Barnhart's arm has declined from great to merely okay over the years, and that his framing has improved from a liability to a clear asset in 2019. Consider also that his DRC+ has finished within a tight 85-90 window in all five of his full seasons. There's something to be said about consistency, even if the area of consistency is substandard. Put another way, if Barnhart's bat were predictably less predictable, he'd probably still be a backup.

YEAR	TEAM	LVL	AGE	PA	DRC+	VORP	BABIP	BRR	FRAA	WARP
2017	CIN	MLB	26	423	90	20.6	.312	-1.6	C(110): 0.7	1.5
2018	CIN	MLB	27	522	86	12.4	.291	-3.3	C(118): -9.6, 1B(11): -0.7	0.2
2019	CIN	MLB	28	364	90	13.8	.278	-3.7	C(102): 15.3, 1B(3): 0.0	2.5
2020	CIN	MLB	29	350	87	8.9	.294	-1.7	C 3	1.2

Tucker Barnhart, continued

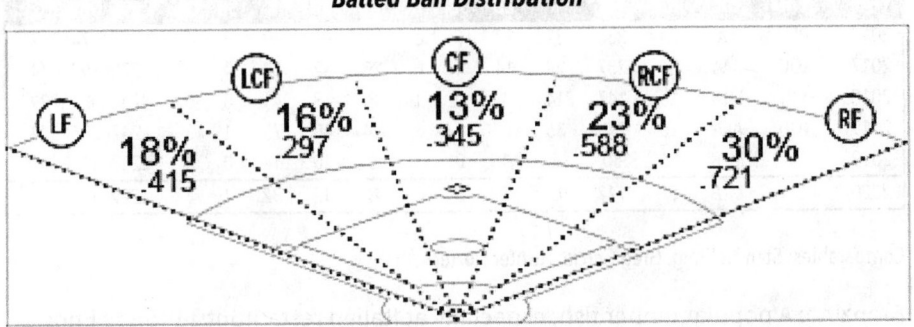

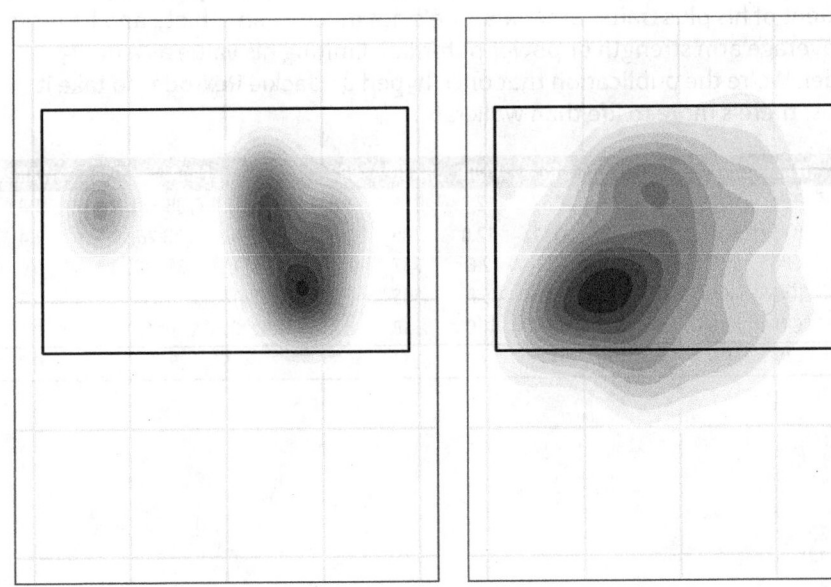

Alex Blandino INF

Born: 11/06/92   Age: 27   Bats: R   Throws: R
Height: 6'0"   Weight: 190   Origin: Round 1, 2014 Draft (#29 overall)

YEAR	TEAM	LVL	AGE	PA	R	2B	3B	HR	RBI	BB	K	SB	CS	AVG/OBP/SLG
2017	PEN	AA	24	236	31	22	0	6	31	32	49	3	4	.259/.374/.462
2017	LOU	AAA	24	237	29	14	1	6	20	32	37	1	3	.270/.390/.444
2018	CIN	MLB	25	147	14	4	0	1	8	13	41	0	0	.234/.324/.289
2019	LOU	AAA	26	293	36	13	1	5	24	40	73	1	3	.247/.386/.372
2019	CIN	MLB	26	50	6	1	0	1	3	10	14	0	0	.250/.420/.361
2020	CIN	MLB	27	112	12	5	0	3	12	12	32	1	1	.229/.335/.379

Comparables: Stan Hollmig, Greg Garcia, Hunter Dozier

Branzino: A popular dinner fish, especially at Italian restaurants. Blonde Eno: Brian in a killer wig. Blandino: a walk-heavy minor-league second baseman. Originally a first-round pick, it seems more likely with each passing month that he'll top out as organizational depth. Blandino's patient, disciplined approach is the extent of his plus traits. Otherwise, he's not much of an athlete and he lacks even average arm strength or power potential, limiting his value as a utility infielder. We're the publication that once hyped up Jackie Rexrode, so take it from us: there's more to life than walk rate.

YEAR	TEAM	LVL	AGE	PA	DRC+	VORP	BABIP	BRR	FRAA	WARP
2017	PEN	AA	24	236	137	12.7	.315	-1.6	2B(39): 1.8, 3B(18): 2.1	1.8
2017	LOU	AAA	24	237	141	12.0	.305	-2.8	2B(29): -1.8, 3B(26): 0.5	1.4
2018	CIN	MLB	25	147	79	2.8	.337	2.3	2B(21): -1.4, 3B(15): -1.2	0.0
2019	LOU	AAA	26	293	108	6.8	.335	-3.2	2B(34): -1.6, SS(18): -1.1	0.8
2019	CIN	MLB	26	50	91	1.0	.348	-0.3	2B(10): 0.1, 3B(4): 0.0	0.1
2020	CIN	MLB	27	112	92	3.0	.311	-0.3	SS 0, 2B -1	0.3

Alex Blandino, continued

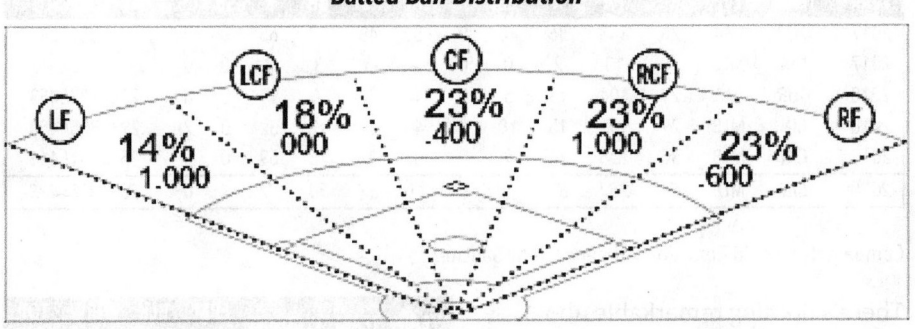

Batted Ball Distribution

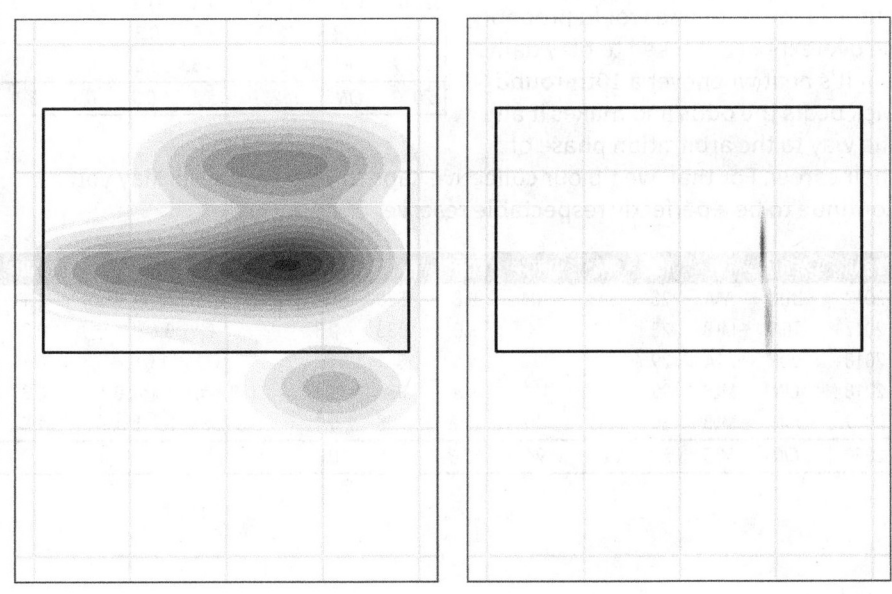

Strike Zone vs LHP   **Strike Zone vs RHP**

Curt Casali C

Born: 11/09/88 Age: 31 Bats: R Throws: R
Height: 6'3" Weight: 225 Origin: Round 10, 2011 Draft (#317 overall)

YEAR	TEAM	LVL	AGE	PA	R	2B	3B	HR	RBI	BB	K	SB	CS	AVG/OBP/SLG
2017	DUR	AAA	28	343	36	10	0	5	48	37	65	0	0	.263/.351/.347
2017	TBA	MLB	28	13	2	0	0	1	3	3	3	0	0	.333/.462/.667
2018	DUR	AAA	29	104	13	5	0	4	20	7	19	0	0	.274/.327/.453
2018	CIN	MLB	29	156	15	10	0	4	16	12	32	0	2	.293/.355/.450
2019	CIN	MLB	30	236	24	9	0	8	32	25	59	0	0	.251/.331/.411
2020	CIN	MLB	31	287	34	13	0	11	37	30	77	1	0	.239/.328/.423

Comparables: David Ross, Chris Gimenez, Tony Sanchez

There's nothing remarkable about Casali's game. He's a good framer and a below-average thrower; a disciplined hitter with pull-side power who strikes out a fair amount and would probably be overexposed if asked to play daily. But it's neat whenever a 10th-round pick beats the odds and makes it all the way to the arbitration phase of their career. For that, we tip our collective caps to you, Mr. Casali. May you continue to be a perfectly respectable reserve.

YEAR	TEAM	P. COUNT	FRM RUNS	BLK RUNS	THRW RUNS	TOT RUNS
2017	DUR	7761	2.3	-3.0	-1.0	-1.7
2017	TBA	486	0.6	-0.1	0.0	0.8
2018	CIN	4795	-2.1	-1.3	-0.2	-3.0
2018	DUR	3527	1.8	0.3	-0.3	1.9
2019	CIN	8388	4.5	1.8	-0.3	6.0
2020	CIN	15231	5.7	-0.3	-0.3	5.1

YEAR	TEAM	LVL	AGE	PA	DRC+	VORP	BABIP	BRR	FRAA	WARP
2017	DUR	AAA	28	343	104	8.8	.320	-0.4	C(53): -2.1	1.1
2017	TBA	MLB	28	13	94	3.0	.333	0.3	C(8): 0.6	0.2
2018	DUR	AAA	29	104	112	4.5	.301	-0.1	C(26): 1.0	0.7
2018	CIN	MLB	29	156	101	9.3	.352	0.1	C(38): -4.1, 1B(6): 0.1	0.3
2019	CIN	MLB	30	236	102	12.8	.308	0.1	C(67): 6.0, 1B(4): 0.0	1.8
2020	CIN	MLB	31	287	98	13.3	.300	0.6	C 5	1.9

Curt Casali, continued

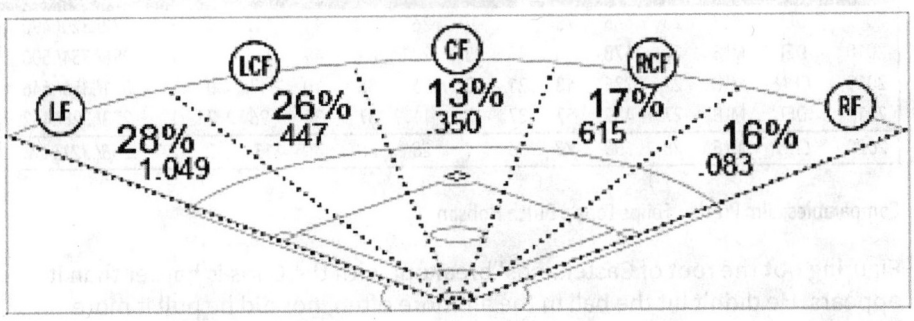

Batted Ball Distribution

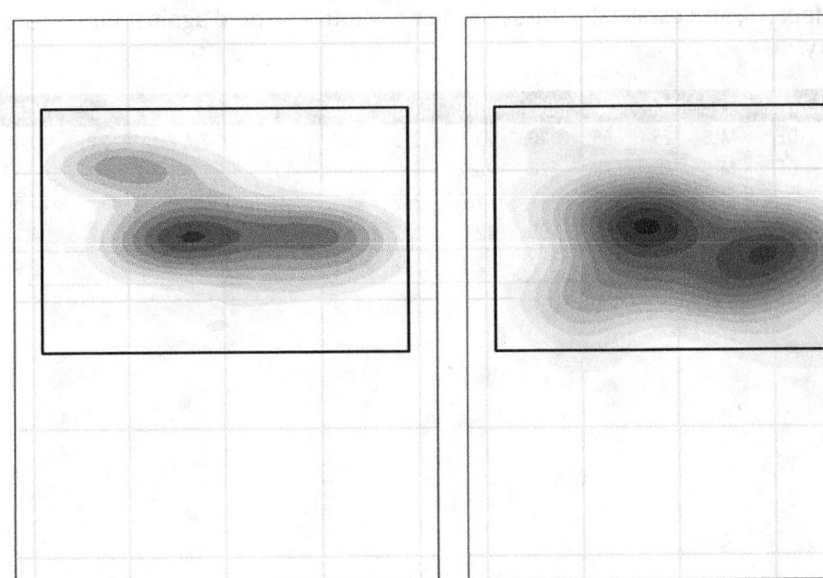

Nicholas Castellanos RF

Born: 03/04/92   Age: 28   Bats: R   Throws: R
Height: 6'4"   Weight: 203   Origin: Round 1, 2010 Draft (#44 overall)

YEAR	TEAM	LVL	AGE	PA	R	2B	3B	HR	RBI	BB	K	SB	CS	AVG/OBP/SLG
2017	DET	MLB	25	665	73	36	10	26	101	41	142	4	5	.272/.320/.490
2018	DET	MLB	26	678	88	46	5	23	89	49	151	2	1	.298/.354/.500
2019	CHN	MLB	27	225	43	21	0	16	36	10	47	0	1	.321/.356/.646
2019	DET	MLB	27	439	57	37	3	11	37	31	96	2	1	.273/.328/.462
2020	CHN	MLB	28	600	73	36	4	28	88	40	134	3	2	.268/.321/.496

Comparables: Jim Presley, Felipe Lopez, Butch Hobson

Figuring out the root of Castellanos' breakout with the Cubs is harder than it appears. He didn't hit the ball in the air more often, nor did he pull it more frequently. He didn't show a greater feel for contact, or demonstrably improve his strike-zone judgement, either. What Castellanos did do was get away from cavernous Comerica Park and a poorly performing team. How much either of those factors, and especially the second one, should be held against him is up to the jury.

YEAR	TEAM	LVL	AGE	PA	DRC+	VORP	BABIP	BRR	FRAA	WARP
2017	DET	MLB	25	665	110	23.2	.313	-2.6	3B(129): -7.7, RF(21): -6.0	1.4
2018	DET	MLB	26	678	124	46.9	.361	3.4	RF(142): -2.8	3.5
2019	CHN	MLB	27	225	141	17.7	.347	0.1	RF(48): 0.9, LF(11): -0.6	1.8
2019	DET	MLB	27	439	105	12.6	.332	-1.7	RF(89): 0.9	1.1
2020	CHN	MLB	28	600	112	12.1	.307	0.1	RF -1, 3B -1	2.9

Nicholas Castellanos, continued

Batted Ball Distribution

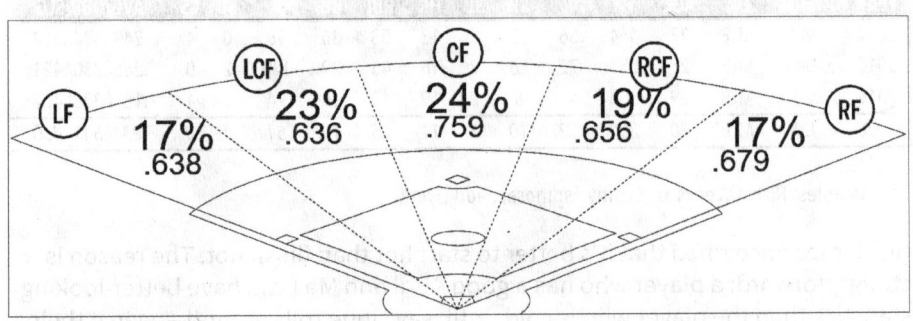

Strike Zone vs LHP

Strike Zone vs RHP

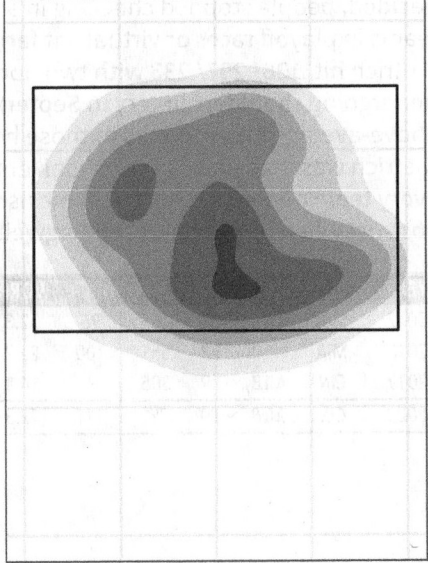

Derek Dietrich 2B

Born: 07/18/89 Age: 30 Bats: L Throws: R
Height: 6'0" Weight: 205 Origin: Round 2, 2010 Draft (#79 overall)

YEAR	TEAM	LVL	AGE	PA	R	2B	3B	HR	RBI	BB	K	SB	CS	AVG/OBP/SLG
2017	MIA	MLB	27	464	56	22	5	13	53	36	98	0	1	.249/.334/.424
2018	MIA	MLB	28	551	72	26	2	16	45	29	140	2	0	.265/.330/.421
2019	CIN	MLB	29	306	41	8	2	19	43	28	74	1	1	.187/.328/.462
2020	CIN	MLB	30	251	32	10	1	11	35	19	61	1	0	.234/.341/.450

Comparables: Rickie Weeks Jr., Danny Espinosa, Jedd Gyorko

Bill James once riffed that it's better to start hot than finish hot. The reason is straightforward: a player who has a good April and May will have better-looking statistics than the player who is cold until, say, June rolls around—even if their production ends up being the same when all is sand and dust. Dietrich is a good example of this in motion. He hit .254/.364/.720 with 17 home runs through May 28th, at which point everyone labeled him a smart get by the Reds. With that decided, people stopped checking in and instead used their time to monitor teams in playoff races or virtual ant farms or whatever. They missed that Dietrich hit .128/.297/.233 with two home runs the rest of the way before undergoing shoulder surgery in September. Despite it all, he still finished as an above-average hitter thanks to those hot months. It didn't matter though. When Dietrich was made available on waivers after the season, before being set free, every team quoted a different Jamesism—the one from the *New Historical Abstract* when he wrote, of Jeff Bagwell, "Pass."

YEAR	TEAM	LVL	AGE	PA	DRC+	VORP	BABIP	BRR	FRAA	WARP
2017	MIA	MLB	27	464	96	22.3	.294	0.5	3B(103): -7.6, 2B(10): 0.3	0.7
2018	MIA	MLB	28	551	100	25.2	.336	1.7	LF(97): -8.4, 1B(33): -1.9	0.4
2019	CIN	MLB	29	306	113	14.1	.176	1.5	2B(58): -3.1, 1B(21): -0.7	1.1
2020	CIN	MLB	30	251	111	12.3	.272	0.6	3B -1, LF -1	1.0

Derek Dietrich, continued

Batted Ball Distribution

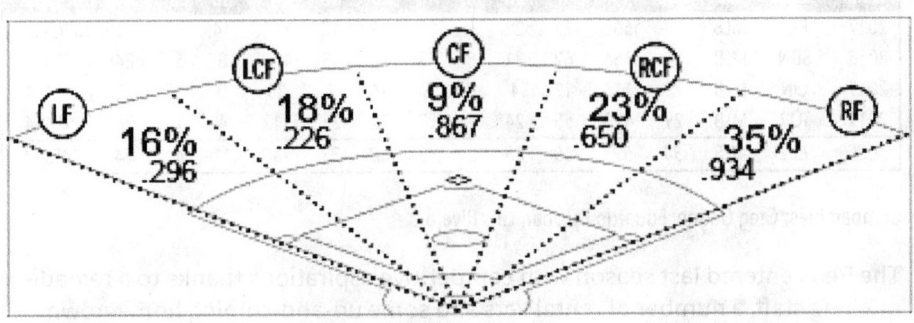

Strike Zone vs LHP

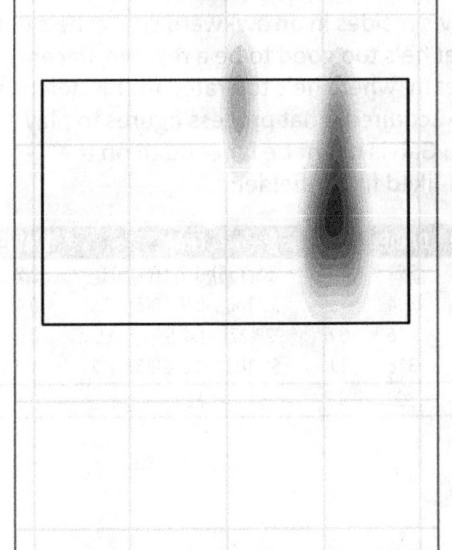

Strike Zone vs RHP

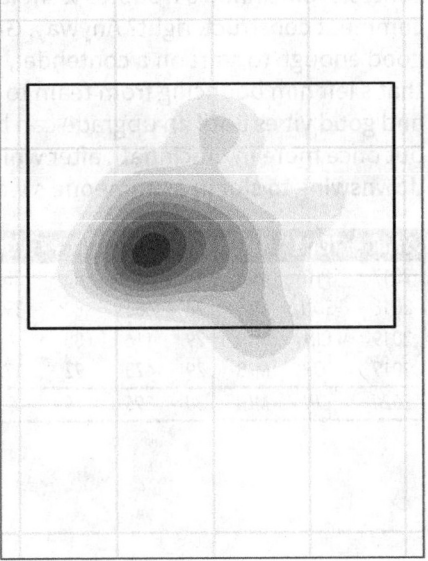

Cincinnati Reds 2020

Freddy Galvis SS
Born: 11/14/89   Age: 30   Bats: B   Throws: R
Height: 5'10"   Weight: 185   Origin: International Free Agent, 2006

YEAR	TEAM	LVL	AGE	PA	R	2B	3B	HR	RBI	BB	K	SB	CS	AVG/OBP/SLG
2017	PHI	MLB	27	663	71	29	6	12	61	45	111	14	5	.255/.309/.382
2018	SDN	MLB	28	656	62	31	5	13	67	45	147	8	6	.248/.299/.380
2019	CIN	MLB	29	116	12	4	0	5	16	7	33	0	1	.234/.284/.411
2019	TOR	MLB	29	473	55	24	1	18	54	21	112	4	1	.267/.299/.444
2020	CIN	MLB	30	595	60	25	2	18	68	33	140	11	4	.248/.292/.397

Comparables: Greg Gagne, Eduardo Escobar, Luis Rivera

The Reds entered last season with competitive aspirations thanks to a remade pitching staff, a number of rental vets and some up-and-coming homegrown talent. It didn't work out. A good microcosm of their season came in late August, when they were swept in a three-game series by the Pirates, who played like a 55-win team during the second half. Galvis batted second in each of those contests. Cincinnati's troubles went far beyond him, but it makes for a nice comment construct, right? Anyway, Galvis resides in an awkward space: he's not good enough to start on a contender, yet he's too good to be a reserve. Recently, that's left him bouncing from team to team, where he's tolerated for his defense and good vibes until an upgrade can be acquired. That process figures to play out once more in Cincinnati, after which Galvis might be far enough on the downswing to slot in as someone's well-liked fifth infielder.

YEAR	TEAM	LVL	AGE	PA	DRC+	VORP	BABIP	BRR	FRAA	WARP
2017	PHI	MLB	27	663	85	25.9	.292	1.6	SS(155): 1.7, LF(1): 0.0	2.2
2018	SDN	MLB	28	656	82	19.0	.304	-1.2	SS(160): -8.9, 2B(5): -0.5	0.4
2019	CIN	MLB	29	116	88	2.2	.286	-0.6	2B(27): -1.4, SS(7): -0.5	0.0
2019	TOR	MLB	29	473	92	17.4	.318	-1.8	SS(103): -2.0, 2B(5): -0.2	1.3
2020	CIN	MLB	30	595	79	5.9	.300	-0.3	SS -3	0.3

Freddy Galvis, continued

Batted Ball Distribution

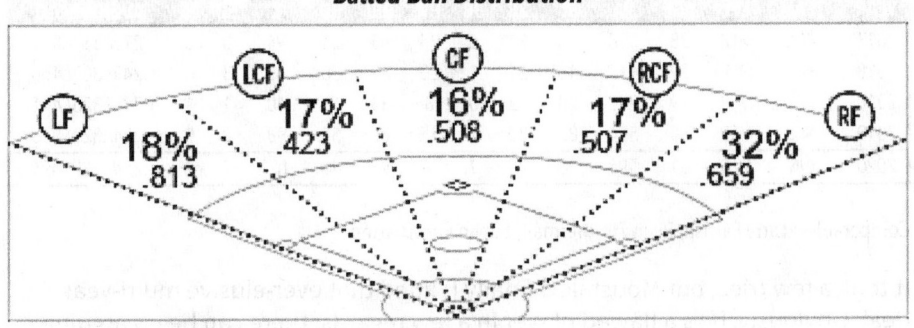

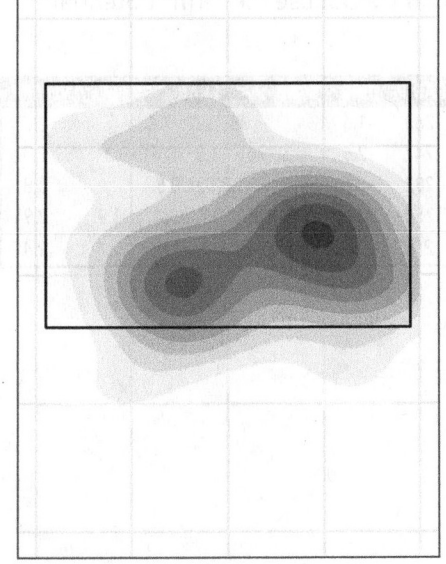

Strike Zone vs LHP

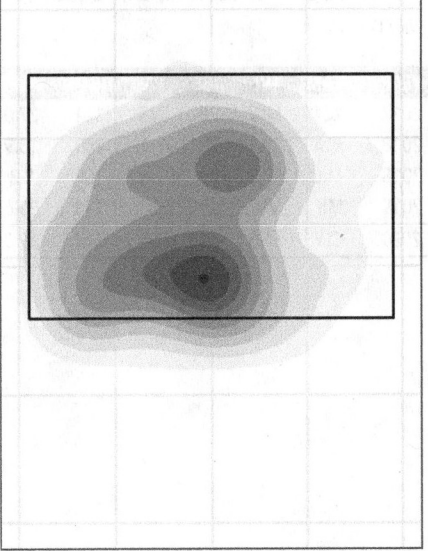

Strike Zone vs RHP

Mike Moustakas 2B

Born: 09/11/88 Age: 31 Bats: L Throws: R
Height: 6'0" Weight: 225 Origin: Round 1, 2007 Draft (#2 overall)

YEAR	TEAM	LVL	AGE	PA	R	2B	3B	HR	RBI	BB	K	SB	CS	AVG/OBP/SLG
2017	KCA	MLB	28	598	75	24	0	38	85	34	94	0	0	.272/.314/.521
2018	KCA	MLB	29	417	46	21	1	20	62	30	63	3	0	.249/.309/.468
2018	MIL	MLB	29	218	20	12	0	8	33	19	40	1	1	.256/.326/.441
2019	MIL	MLB	30	584	80	30	1	35	87	53	98	3	0	.254/.329/.516
2020	CIN	MLB	31	595	78	28	1	34	93	48	101	2	1	.254/.322/.496

Comparables: Larry Parrish, Ryan Zimmerman, Edwin Encarnación

It took a few tries, but Moustakas finally landed that ever-elusive multi-year deal. Obviously, he's a flawed player in a few regards; there can be no arguing that, especially in the face of four consecutive seasons with an OBP under .330, poor base running and middling defense. But *sheesh*. In past editions, we might have dunked on the Reds for the potential overpay. These days, with the state of baseball being what it is, we're just glad that we can use the term "potential overpay."

YEAR	TEAM	LVL	AGE	PA	DRC+	VORP	BABIP	BRR	FRAA	WARP
2017	KCA	MLB	28	598	121	27.0	.263	-1.6	3B(127): -7.4	2.7
2018	KCA	MLB	29	417	109	13.9	.247	-2.6	3B(76): 11.3, 1B(4): -0.2	2.7
2018	MIL	MLB	29	218	107	8.3	.282	-2.6	3B(52): 0.5	0.8
2019	MIL	MLB	30	584	118	35.6	.250	-2.8	3B(105): -0.7, 2B(47): -1.9	2.9
2020	CIN	MLB	31	595	111	29.3	.255	-2.9	2B -7, 3B 0	2.4

Mike Moustakas, continued

Batted Ball Distribution

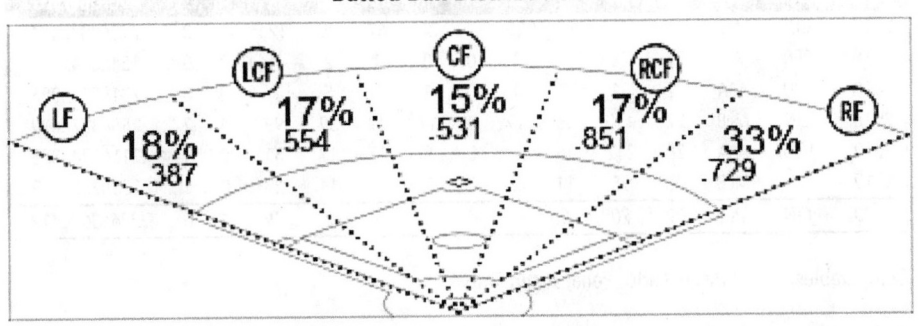

Strike Zone vs LHP   **Strike Zone vs RHP**

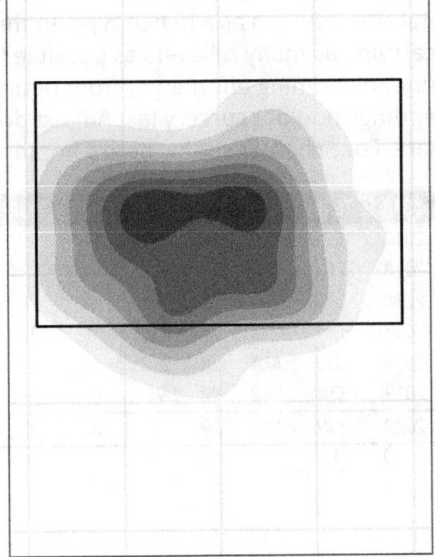

Scott Schebler OF

Born: 10/06/90   Age: 29   Bats: L   Throws: R
Height: 6'0"   Weight: 228   Origin: Round 26, 2010 Draft (#802 overall)

YEAR	TEAM	LVL	AGE	PA	R	2B	3B	HR	RBI	BB	K	SB	CS	AVG/OBP/SLG
2017	CIN	MLB	26	531	63	25	2	30	67	39	125	5	3	.233/.307/.484
2018	PEN	AA	27	28	2	1	0	0	1	2	4	0	0	.154/.214/.192
2018	LOU	AAA	27	31	3	1	0	1	2	5	6	0	0	.231/.355/.385
2018	CIN	MLB	27	430	55	19	0	17	49	39	99	4	2	.255/.337/.439
2019	LOU	AAA	28	212	18	6	0	5	17	12	51	0	1	.216/.274/.325
2019	CIN	MLB	28	95	11	2	0	2	7	14	27	0	1	.123/.253/.222
2020	CIN	MLB	29	70	8	3	0	3	9	5	19	1	0	.226/.300/.412

Comparables: Eric Munson, Carlos Pena, Justin Smoak

Schebler has virtues, but each comes with a caveat: he can start most days, yet he needs to sit against lefties; he can cover center adequately for periods of time, even if he's not great at it; he's a decent hitter, though his DRC+ has topped 100 just once; and so on. Fifteen years ago, he would've enjoyed a decade-long run as a bench type. In this era, where teams are obsessive about carrying as many relievers as possible? Schebler is probably another underwhelming effort away from permanent residence in Triple-A. Season-ending shoulder surgery last August doesn't help his chances of avoiding that fate. For Schebler's sake, here's hoping he comes back hearty and hale.

YEAR	TEAM	LVL	AGE	PA	DRC+	VORP	BABIP	BRR	FRAA	WARP
2017	CIN	MLB	26	531	95	20.3	.248	-0.2	RF(120): -4.8, CF(15): 0.9	0.5
2018	PEN	AA	27	28	47	-2.0	.182	0.0	RF(6): -1.0, LF(1): -0.1	-0.2
2018	LOU	AAA	27	31	100	1.1	.263	0.0	LF(1): 0.1, RF(1): 0.1	0.1
2018	CIN	MLB	27	430	101	15.3	.301	-1.4	RF(86): -2.4, CF(16): 0.5	0.7
2019	LOU	AAA	28	212	52	-11.9	.264	-1.7	CF(33): -0.9, LF(9): 1.5	-0.6
2019	CIN	MLB	28	95	67	-0.6	.154	0.1	CF(24): 0.8, LF(3): -0.1	0.0
2020	CIN	MLB	29	70	85	0.1	.281	-0.1	RF -1	-0.1

Scott Schebler, continued

Batted Ball Distribution

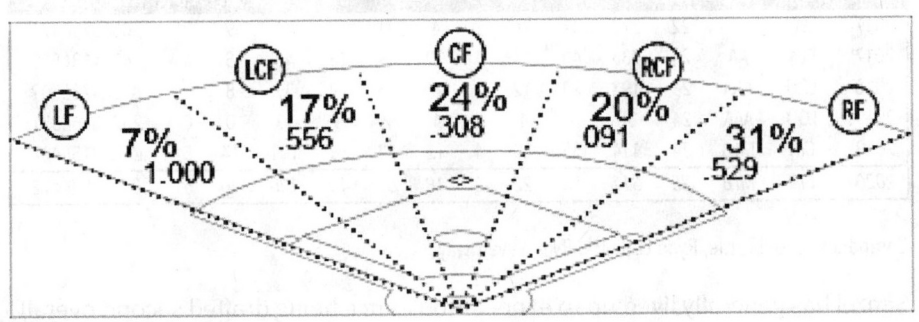

Strike Zone vs LHP   Strike Zone vs RHP

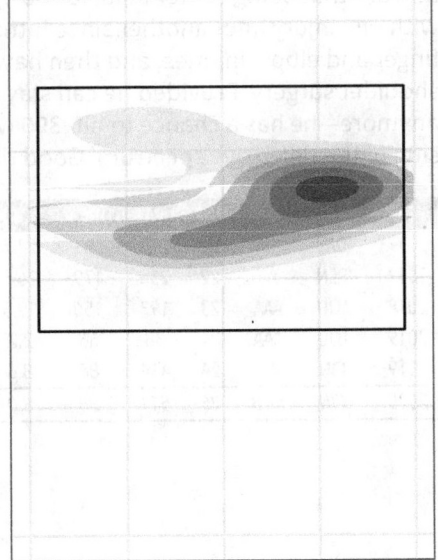

Nick Senzel CF

Born: 06/29/95 Age: 25 Bats: R Throws: R
Height: 6'1" Weight: 205 Origin: Round 1, 2016 Draft (#2 overall)

YEAR	TEAM	LVL	AGE	PA	R	2B	3B	HR	RBI	BB	K	SB	CS	AVG/OBP/SLG
2017	DAY	A+	22	272	41	26	2	4	31	23	54	9	2	.305/.371/.476
2017	PEN	AA	22	235	40	14	1	10	34	26	43	5	4	.340/.413/.560
2018	LOU	AAA	23	193	23	12	2	6	25	19	39	8	2	.310/.378/.509
2019	LOU	AAA	24	38	7	1	0	1	2	3	13	0	0	.257/.316/.371
2019	CIN	MLB	24	414	55	20	4	12	42	30	101	14	5	.256/.315/.427
2020	CIN	MLB	25	511	56	22	2	18	62	40	128	10	5	.242/.307/.412

Comparables: Bill Tuttle, Ryan Ludwick, Ryan Lavarnway

Senzel has generally lived up to expectations since being drafted second overall a few years back. He pairs plus contact skills with good but not great power and a mature enough understanding of the zone. On paper, he profiles as a well-rounded, safe big-league starter at whatever position the Reds choose to stick him at—that being center field, for now, anyway. Unfortunately, Senzel has dealt with one injury after another since hitting pro ball, losing chunks of 2018 to finger and elbow injuries, and then having his 2019 end early due to right shoulder surgery. Provided he can stay on the field—and who knows anymore—he has a chance to hit .300 while playing a position on the valuable side of the defensive spectrum. Good player.

YEAR	TEAM	LVL	AGE	PA	DRC+	VORP	BABIP	BRR	FRAA	WARP
2017	DAY	A+	22	272	161	24.7	.378	1.3	3B(60): 5.1	3.0
2017	PEN	AA	22	235	179	26.6	.391	-0.5	3B(56): 1.7	2.8
2018	LOU	AAA	23	193	156	19.5	.367	1.9	2B(28): -0.8, 3B(14): 0.8	1.8
2019	LOU	AAA	24	38	66	2.2	.381	0.4	CF(8): -1.2	-0.1
2019	CIN	MLB	24	414	88	8.6	.319	-0.1	CF(96): -4.6, 2B(1): 0.0	0.4
2020	CIN	MLB	25	511	88	8.0	.296	-0.4	LF, CF -3	0.5

Nick Senzel, continued

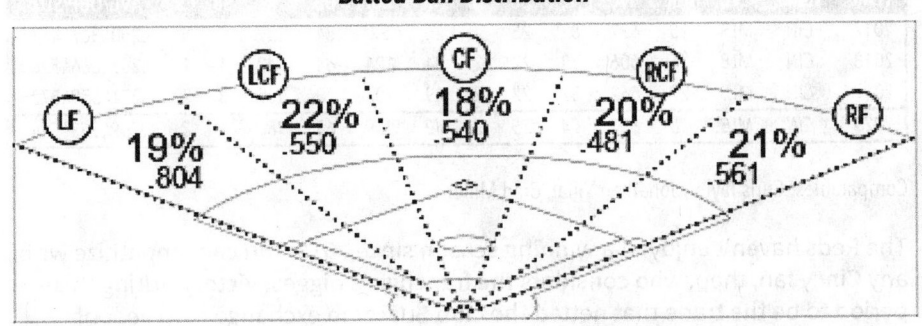

Strike Zone vs LHP **Strike Zone vs RHP**

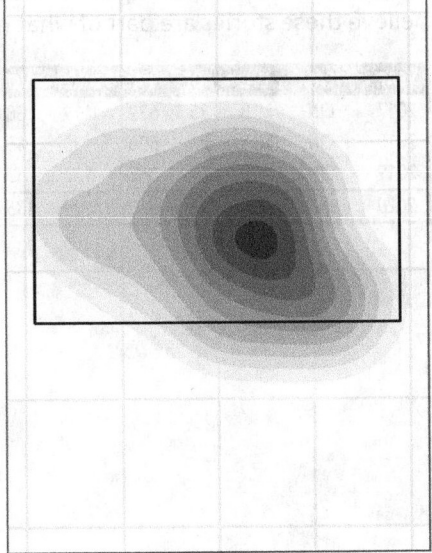

Eugenio Suárez 3B

Born: 07/18/91   Age: 28   Bats: R   Throws: R
Height: 5'11"   Weight: 213   Origin: International Free Agent, 2008

YEAR	TEAM	LVL	AGE	PA	R	2B	3B	HR	RBI	BB	K	SB	CS	AVG/OBP/SLG
2017	CIN	MLB	25	632	87	25	2	26	82	84	147	4	5	.260/.367/.461
2018	CIN	MLB	26	606	79	22	2	34	104	64	142	1	1	.283/.366/.526
2019	CIN	MLB	27	662	87	22	2	49	103	70	189	3	2	.271/.358/.572
2020	CIN	MLB	28	630	94	25	2	42	109	63	180	6	3	.269/.353/.544

Comparables: Chris Taylor, Jonathan Villar, Brad Miller

The Reds haven't enjoyed a winning season since 2013. You can empathize with any Cincy fan, then, who considers the franchise's biggest victory during this period to be the trade that netted the club Suárez in exchange for a year of Alfredo Simon. Top prospect lists gravitate toward recent first-round draft picks and J2 bonus babies, but sometimes players like Suárez—who was neither—end up more valuable by virtue of constant, reliable improvement. We'd tsk-tsk ourselves for never thinking Suárez would be this good, yet the truth is we believe these stories are part of what makes the game so great.

YEAR	TEAM	LVL	AGE	PA	DRC+	VORP	BABIP	BRR	FRAA	WARP
2017	CIN	MLB	25	632	119	38.0	.309	-4.7	3B(153): -1.9, SS(1): 0.0	3.2
2018	CIN	MLB	26	606	136	46.2	.322	-3.5	3B(143): -7.6, SS(3): 0.0	3.8
2019	CIN	MLB	27	662	132	53.3	.312	-7.9	3B(158): 0.1	4.4
2020	CIN	MLB	28	630	130	35.6	.323	-4.4	3B -3	3.4

Eugenio Suárez, continued

Batted Ball Distribution

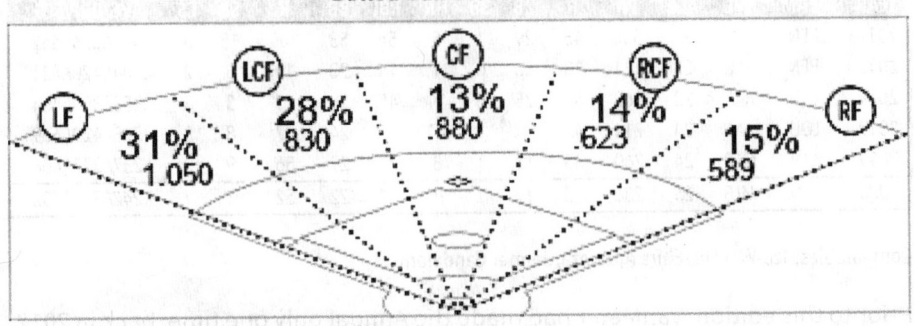

Strike Zone vs LHP

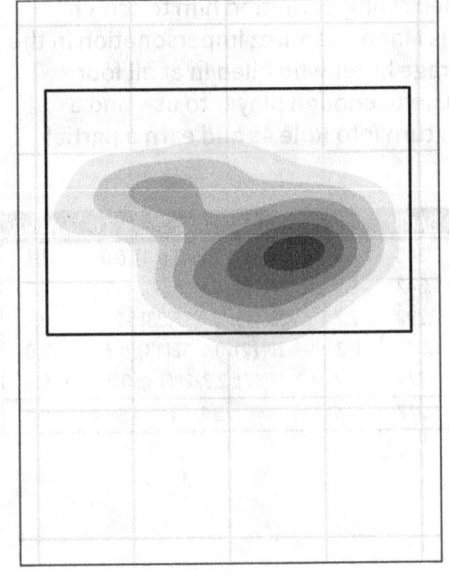

Strike Zone vs RHP

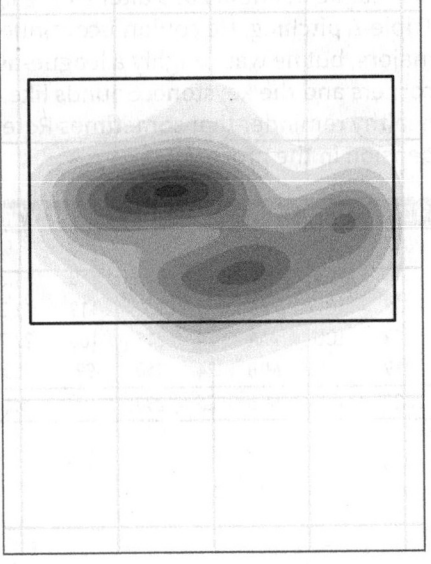

Josh VanMeter UT

Born: 03/10/95 Age: 25 Bats: L Throws: R
Height: 5'11" Weight: 165 Origin: Round 5, 2013 Draft (#148 overall)

YEAR	TEAM	LVL	AGE	PA	R	2B	3B	HR	RBI	BB	K	SB	CS	AVG/OBP/SLG
2017	PEN	AA	22	538	45	29	1	5	54	53	100	15	3	.255/.326/.352
2018	PEN	AA	23	121	13	10	0	1	14	23	19	5	2	.284/.420/.421
2018	LOU	AAA	23	362	40	25	6	11	45	28	73	5	3	.253/.309/.464
2019	LOU	AAA	24	211	43	14	1	14	43	24	37	8	3	.348/.429/.669
2019	CIN	MLB	24	260	33	13	1	8	23	29	56	9	3	.237/.327/.408
2020	CIN	MLB	25	238	28	11	1	10	31	22	52	3	1	.242/.316/.432

Comparables: Tzu-Wei Lin, Ehire Adrianza, Jeimer Candelario

Prior to this edition, VanMeter had made the Annual only one time: back in 2017, when we noted he had shown "plus power and strong plate discipline," in High-A. He struggled in a subsequent promotion to Double-A, and was later traded from the Padres to the Reds. A few years have passed, yet VanMeter made his big-league debut in 2019 after a redesigned swing permitted him to scorch Triple-A pitching. He couldn't continue his Manny Ramirez impersonation in the majors, but he was roughly a league-average hitter who filled in at all four corners and the keystone. Sounds like a useful enough player to us—and a healthy reminder that sometimes Role 3s turn into Role 4s and earn a partial pension in the process.

YEAR	TEAM	LVL	AGE	PA	DRC+	VORP	BABIP	BRR	FRAA	WARP
2017	PEN	AA	22	538	103	8.0	.308	-0.5	3B(48): -2.5, 2B(41): 0.0	1.1
2018	PEN	AA	23	121	150	11.3	.342	-0.4	LF(15): -0.9, 2B(9): -0.4	0.7
2018	LOU	AAA	23	362	113	11.3	.292	-2.7	2B(47): -3.8, LF(23): -1.3	0.8
2019	LOU	AAA	24	211	160	27.7	.371	0.2	2B(22): 0.1, 1B(13): 0.4	2.0
2019	CIN	MLB	24	260	99	7.0	.279	-1.2	LF(47): 2.3, 2B(18): 0.2	0.8
2020	CIN	MLB	25	238	95	5.1	.277	-0.6	1B 2, 2B 0	0.6

Josh VanMeter, continued

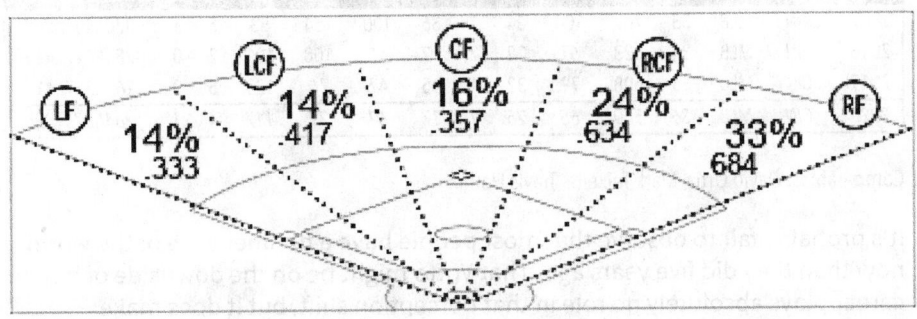

Batted Ball Distribution

Strike Zone vs LHP

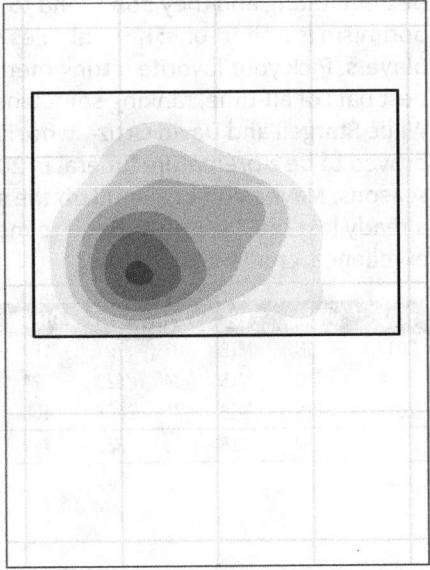

Strike Zone vs RHP

Joey Votto 1B

Born: 09/10/83   Age: 36   Bats: L   Throws: R
Height: 6'2"   Weight: 220   Origin: Round 2, 2002 Draft (#44 overall)

YEAR	TEAM	LVL	AGE	PA	R	2B	3B	HR	RBI	BB	K	SB	CS	AVG/OBP/SLG
2017	CIN	MLB	33	707	106	34	1	36	100	134	83	5	1	.320/.454/.578
2018	CIN	MLB	34	623	67	28	2	12	67	108	101	2	0	.284/.417/.419
2019	CIN	MLB	35	608	79	32	1	15	47	76	123	5	0	.261/.357/.411
2020	CIN	MLB	36	560	68	25	1	17	67	79	117	4	1	.264/.374/.428

Comparables: David Ortiz, Mark Teixeira, Travis Hafner

It's probably fair to observe that most people have a dimmer view of the world now than they did five years ago. That Votto might be on the downside of his career plays absolutely no role in that perception shift, but it does make baseball less enjoyable. Votto has had a bad season before—in 2014, he played in 62 games before he was shelved with a left knee/quad injury. He was injured again last year, this time it was his back ailing him. Back injuries, obviously, can be debilitating and they don't tend to improve as you age. The argument for optimism is a short one: normal rules don't apply to Hall of Fame-caliber players. Pick your favorite hitting metric and Votto has been one of the 30 or 40 best bats of all-time, ranking somewhere in the vicinity of say, Willie McCovey, Willie Stargell and David Ortiz—who, it should be noted, recovered from what proved to be a premature funeral in 2009 and turned in another seven good seasons. Maybe Votto can pull off the same trick. Hopefully he does. We've already lost the Zac Brown Band to mediocrity, let us have some more Votto excellence, cruel world. Please?

YEAR	TEAM	LVL	AGE	PA	DRC+	VORP	BABIP	BRR	FRAA	WARP
2017	CIN	MLB	33	707	159	69.0	.321	-6.9	1B(162): 9.5	6.5
2018	CIN	MLB	34	623	124	29.2	.333	-2.6	1B(139): 11.6	3.7
2019	CIN	MLB	35	608	108	16.2	.313	-4.3	1B(133): 4.6	1.6
2020	CIN	MLB	36	560	114	17.3	.317	-3.7	1B 11	2.9

Joey Votto, continued

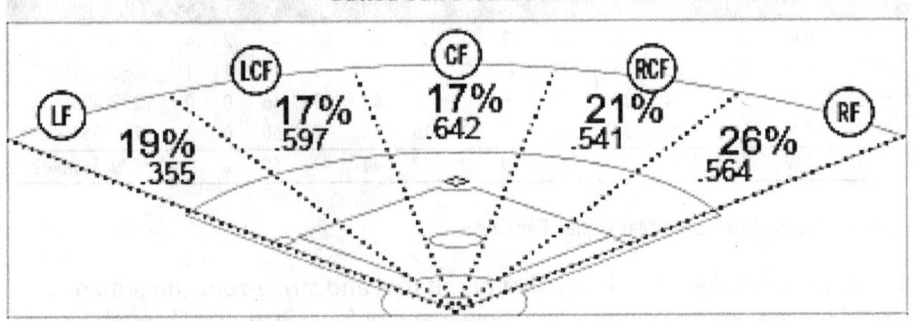

Batted Ball Distribution

Strike Zone vs LHP   **Strike Zone vs RHP**

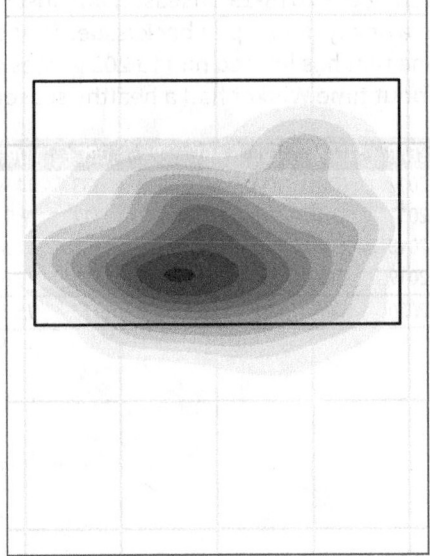

Jesse Winker   OF

Born: 08/17/93   Age: 26   Bats: L   Throws: L
Height: 6'3"   Weight: 215   Origin: Round 1, 2012 Draft (#49 overall)

YEAR	TEAM	LVL	AGE	PA	R	2B	3B	HR	RBI	BB	K	SB	CS	AVG/OBP/SLG
2017	LOU	AAA	23	347	33	22	0	2	41	38	46	2	4	.314/.395/.408
2017	CIN	MLB	23	137	21	7	0	7	15	15	24	1	1	.298/.375/.529
2018	CIN	MLB	24	334	38	16	0	7	43	49	46	0	0	.299/.405/.431
2019	CIN	MLB	25	384	51	17	2	16	38	38	60	0	2	.269/.357/.473
2020	CIN	MLB	26	357	43	18	0	12	44	41	59	2	1	.270/.361/.442

Comparables: Andruw Jones, Max Kepler, Ben Grieve

The book on Winker was always that his hit tool and strike-zone judgement would have to atone for his lacking power and defensive utility. Through his age-25 season, that's mostly been the case—and he's been quite productive, as an above-average hitter. So why then has his career felt underwhelming? Likely because of unforeseen injury woes. Winker had to undergo shoulder surgery during the 2018-19 offseason and just missed the second half of the season due to a newly developed back issue. That's a bad combination, to say the least, and one that has limited him to 202 games over the past two seasons. Now 26, it's about time Winker had a healthy season.

YEAR	TEAM	LVL	AGE	PA	DRC+	VORP	BABIP	BRR	FRAA	WARP
2017	LOU	AAA	23	347	133	14.9	.359	-3.2	RF(70): 2.7, LF(3): 0.4	1.8
2017	CIN	MLB	23	137	112	9.5	.322	-0.6	RF(25): -1.4, LF(2): -0.3	0.3
2018	CIN	MLB	24	334	118	17.5	.336	-2.6	RF(47): -1.0, LF(34): -3.5	0.8
2019	CIN	MLB	25	384	115	18.6	.286	0.6	LF(72): 1.4, CF(21): 0.0	2.2
2020	CIN	MLB	26	357	113	15.1	.301	-0.6	LF -2	1.3

Jesse Winker, continued

Batted Ball Distribution

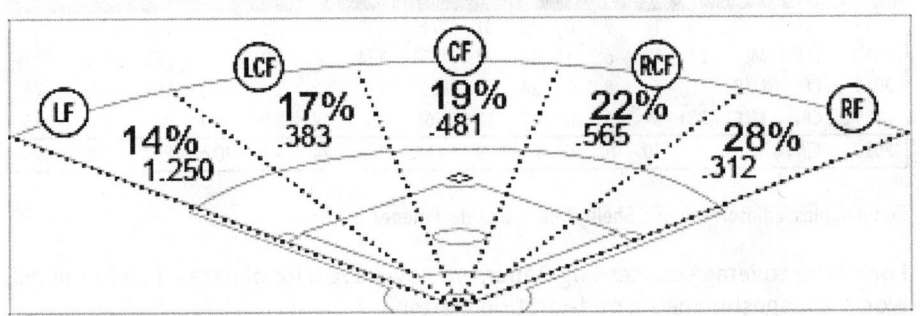

Strike Zone vs LHP   Strike Zone vs RHP

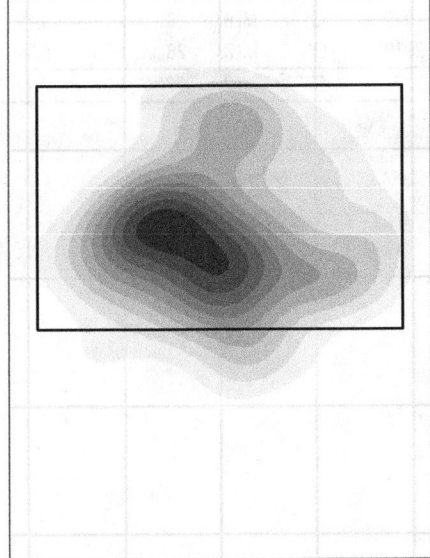

Trevor Bauer RHP

Born: 01/17/91 Age: 29 Bats: R Throws: R
Height: 6'1" Weight: 205 Origin: Round 1, 2011 Draft (#3 overall)

YEAR	TEAM	LVL	AGE	W	L	SV	G	GS	IP	H	HR	BB/9	K/9	K	GB%	BABIP
2017	CLE	MLB	26	17	9	0	32	31	176^1	181	25	3.1	10.0	196	47%	.337
2018	CLE	MLB	27	12	6	1	28	27	175^1	134	9	2.9	11.3	221	45%	.297
2019	CLE	MLB	28	9	8	0	24	24	156^2	127	22	3.6	10.6	185	40%	.276
2019	CIN	MLB	28	2	5	0	10	10	56^1	57	12	3.0	10.9	68	36%	.315
2020	CIN	MLB	29	10	10	0	29	29	172	150	24	3.6	10.6	202	40%	.294

Comparables: Edinson Vólquez, Shelby Miller, Ubaldo Jiménez

For all the coverage concerning Bauer, we now have a lot of data—1,117 innings' worth—suggesting he's a mid-rotation starter.

YEAR	TEAM	LVL	AGE	WHIP	ERA	DRA	WARP	MPH	FB%	WHF	CSP
2017	CLE	MLB	26	1.37	4.19	3.95	3.2	96.4	49.3	10.1	44
2018	CLE	MLB	27	1.09	2.21	2.48	5.7	96.8	42.2	14.2	44.3
2019	CLE	MLB	28	1.21	3.79	4.67	1.9	96.8	45.3	13.2	44.2
2019	CIN	MLB	28	1.35	6.39	5.53	0.1	96.0	45.3	13.5	44.2
2020	CIN	MLB	29	1.27	3.92	3.99	3.5	95.9	45.3	12.8	44.2

Trevor Bauer, continued

Pitch Shape vs LHH

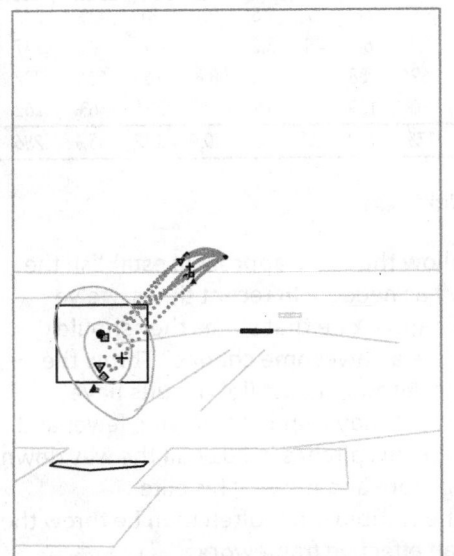

Pitch Shape vs RHH

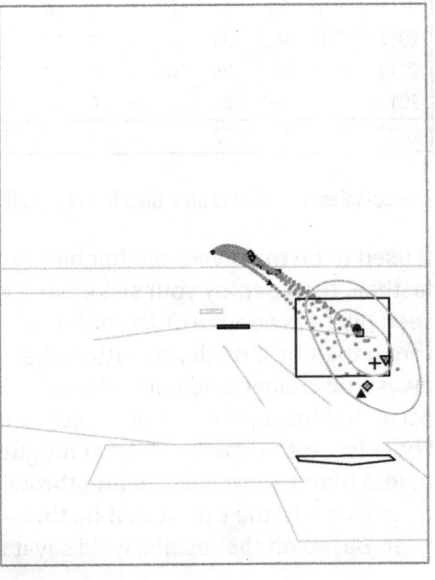

Type	Frequency	Velocity	H Movement	V Movement
● Fastball	38.3%	94.8 [107]	-8.3 [94]	-12.2 [110]
☐ Sinker	4.0%	95.1 [113]	-13.9 [92]	-17 [112]
+ Cutter	16.5%	84.9 [76]	5.3 [120]	-35.4 [58]
▲ Changeup	7.6%	86.3 [104]	-13.4 [90]	-25.1 [107]
✕ Splitter				
▽ Slider	13.9%	79.8 [81]	17 [150]	-40.8 [78]
◇ Curveball	19.8%	79.4 [103]	7.6 [101]	-56.3 [82]
⊕ Slow Curveball				
✱ Knuckleball				
▼ Screwball				

Luis Castillo   RHP

Born: 12/12/92   Age: 27   Bats: R   Throws: R
Height: 6'2"   Weight: 190   Origin: International Free Agent, 2012

YEAR	TEAM	LVL	AGE	W	L	SV	G	GS	IP	H	HR	BB/9	K/9	K	GB%	BABIP
2017	PEN	AA	24	4	4	0	14	14	80^1	68	5	1.5	9.1	81	42%	.293
2017	CIN	MLB	24	3	7	0	15	15	89^1	64	11	3.2	9.9	98	60%	.247
2018	CIN	MLB	25	10	12	0	31	31	169^2	158	28	2.6	8.8	165	48%	.282
2019	CIN	MLB	26	15	8	0	32	32	190^2	139	22	3.7	10.7	226	56%	.262
2020	CIN	MLB	27	11	10	0	29	29	175	142	22	3.8	10.9	212	55%	.286

Comparables: Vince Velasquez, Brandon Woodruff, Nick Pivetta

It used to be that every pitcher had to follow the same approach: establish the fastball, then deploy your secondary stuff as needed. In recent times, we've seen pitchers adapt a different line of thinking—one that states they should throw their best pitch no matter what. Have an awesome change? Throw the awesome change and enjoy the easy outs. Although Castillo's results have oscillated from year to year, he continued a steady trend of throwing fewer and fewer four-seam fastballs (from roughly half his pitches in 2017 all the way down to less than a third in 2019) and throwing more and more of his elite changeup—to the extent that he threw the cambio more often than he threw the heat. Based on the results, we'd say it's an effective framework.

YEAR	TEAM	LVL	AGE	WHIP	ERA	DRA	WARP	MPH	FB%	WHF	CSP
2017	PEN	AA	24	1.01	2.58	3.47	1.6				
2017	CIN	MLB	24	1.07	3.12	3.41	2.2	99.1	62.1	13.5	47.9
2018	CIN	MLB	25	1.22	4.30	4.76	1.1	98.2	57.2	14.2	48.9
2019	CIN	MLB	26	1.14	3.40	3.02	5.7	98.3	50.6	16.7	40.1
2020	CIN	MLB	27	1.23	3.35	3.48	4.5	97.9	55.3	15.5	45.6

Luis Castillo, continued

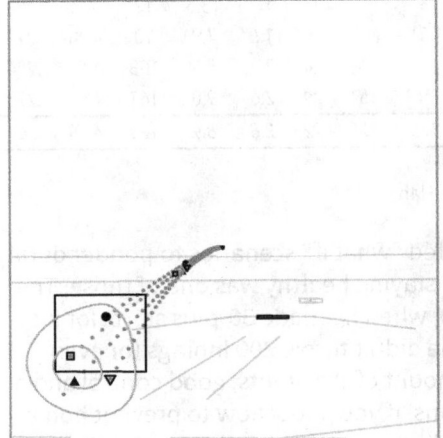
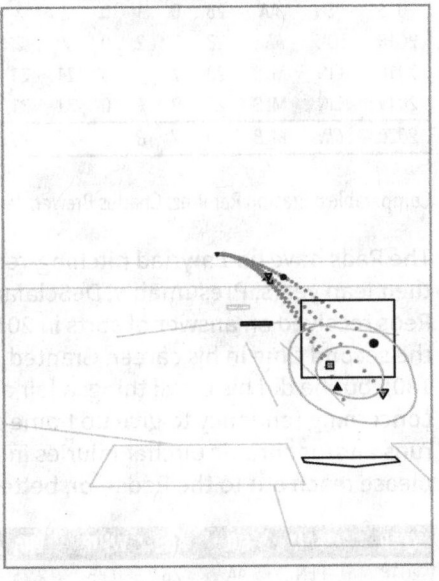

Type	Frequency	Velocity	H Movement	V Movement
● Fastball	29.9%	96.5 [112]	-11 [82]	-16.1 [100]
☐ Sinker	20.7%	96.6 [121]	-15.7 [80]	-22.2 [93]
+ Cutter				
▲ Changeup	32.5%	87.3 [107]	-14.1 [86]	-29.9 [93]
✕ Splitter				
▽ Slider	17.0%	85.9 [107]	0.1 [80]	-32.8 [101]
◇ Curveball				
✦ Slow Curveball				
✳ Knuckleball				
▼ Screwball				

Anthony DeSclafani   RHP
Born: 04/18/90   Age: 30   Bats: R   Throws: R
Height: 6'1"   Weight: 195   Origin: Round 6, 2011 Draft (#199 overall)

YEAR	TEAM	LVL	AGE	W	L	SV	G	GS	IP	H	HR	BB/9	K/9	K	GB%	BABIP
2018	PEN	AA	28	0	1	0	2	2	8	5	0	1.1	13.5	12	59%	.294
2018	LOU	AAA	28	0	2	0	2	2	11^1	15	5	1.6	7.9	10	43%	.312
2018	CIN	MLB	28	7	8	0	21	21	115	118	24	2.3	8.5	108	43%	.294
2019	CIN	MLB	29	9	9	0	31	31	166^2	151	29	2.6	9.0	167	44%	.273
2020	CIN	MLB	30	7	8	0	23	23	125	125	22	2.8	8.9	123	43%	.301

Comparables: Erasmo Ramírez, Charles Brewer, Jesse Hahn

The Reds have had myriad pitching-related "what if" scenarios to ponder during their lean years. Presumably, DeSclafani staying healthy was one of those. The Reds received an answer of sorts in 2019, when he made 30-plus starts for just the second time in his career. Granted, he didn't throw 200 innings (or even 180), but he did his usual thing: a fair amount of strikeouts, good control and a concerning tendency to give up home runs. If you know how to prevent home runs and/or chronic pitcher injuries in otherwise capable mid-rotation starters, please reach out to the Reds—or, better yet, to this author.

YEAR	TEAM	LVL	AGE	WHIP	ERA	DRA	WARP	MPH	FB%	WHF	CSP
2018	PEN	AA	28	0.75	2.25	2.42	0.3				
2018	LOU	AAA	28	1.50	6.35	6.91	-0.2				
2018	CIN	MLB	28	1.29	4.93	5.16	0.2	96.0	57.9	10.7	49.8
2019	CIN	MLB	29	1.20	3.89	3.95	3.3	96.4	55.4	11.3	46.2
2020	CIN	MLB	30	1.31	4.39	4.49	1.8	95.5	56.1	11	47.7

Anthony DeSclafani, continued

Pitch Shape vs LHH

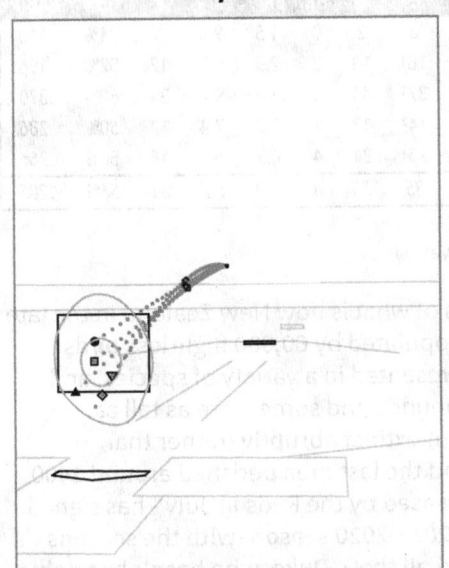

Pitch Shape vs RHH

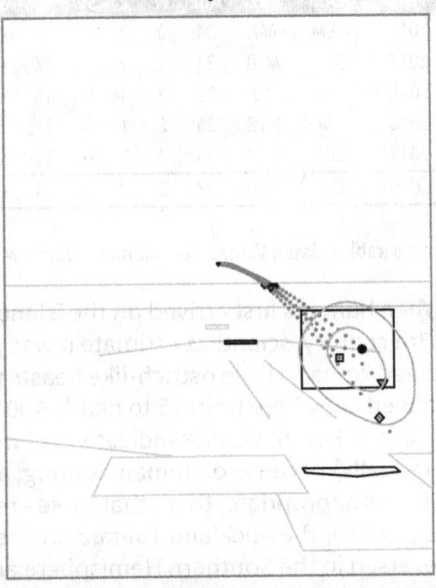

Type	Frequency	Velocity	H Movement	V Movement
● Fastball	37.0%	95 [107]	-8.2 [94]	-12.8 [108]
☐ Sinker	18.4%	94.7 [111]	-13 [98]	-17.3 [111]
+ Cutter				
▲ Changeup	5.3%	88.6 [112]	-11.8 [97]	-25.4 [106]
✕ Splitter				
▽ Slider	25.3%	89.5 [121]	3.7 [95]	-24.5 [125]
◇ Curveball	14.0%	83.3 [116]	4.6 [88]	-40.1 [116]
⊕ Slow Curveball				
✷ Knuckleball				
▼ Screwball				

Cincinnati Reds 2020

Zach Duke LHP
Born: 04/19/83 Age: 37 Bats: L Throws: L
Height: 6'2" Weight: 210 Origin: Round 20, 2001 Draft (#594 overall)

YEAR	TEAM	LVL	AGE	W	L	SV	G	GS	IP	H	HR	BB/9	K/9	K	GB%	BABIP
2017	MEM	AAA	34	0	0	0	6	0	6	2	0	1.5	9.0	6	71%	.143
2017	SLN	MLB	34	1	1	0	27	0	18^1	13	3	2.9	5.9	12	52%	.196
2018	MIN	MLB	35	3	4	0	45	0	37^1	44	0	3.6	9.4	39	60%	.370
2018	SEA	MLB	35	2	1	0	27	0	14^2	13	1	3.7	7.4	12	60%	.286
2019	CIN	MLB	36	3	1	0	30	0	23^1	21	4	6.9	6.9	18	50%	.266
2020	CIN	MLB	37	2	2	0	33	0	35	33	4	4.0	8.0	31	56%	.285

Comparables: Jason Vargas, Joe Saunders, Jamie Moyer

When humans first arrived on the islands of what is now New Zealand in the late 13th century, scientists estimate it was populated by 60,000 flightless birds called "moa." These ostrich-like beasts presented in a variety of species, and ranged anywhere from 25 to nearly 600 pounds and some were as tall as 6-foot-5. Recent studies indicate they went extinct abruptly (rather than gradually) because of human hunting, and the last moa perished around 1400 CE. It is appropriate, then, that Duke - released by the Reds in July - has signed to pitch for the Auckland Tuatara for the 2019-2020 season (with the seasons reversed in the Southern Hemisphere and all that). Duke, who hasn't been able to get right-handed batters out for some time now, may want to read up on the moa during his stay. He and his LOOGY peers are about to become the baseball equivalent with the three-batter minimum rule in place.

YEAR	TEAM	LVL	AGE	WHIP	ERA	DRA	WARP	MPH	FB%	WHF	CSP
2017	MEM	AAA	34	0.50	0.00	2.22	0.2				
2017	SLN	MLB	34	1.04	3.93	5.47	-0.1	89.8	57.3	13	47.9
2018	MIN	MLB	35	1.58	3.62	3.73	0.5	90.2	47.2	10.9	45.8
2018	SEA	MLB	35	1.30	5.52	3.65	0.2	90.8	53.9	11	43.7
2019	CIN	MLB	36	1.67	5.01	7.13	-0.5	91.0	56	9.3	41.7
2020	CIN	MLB	37	1.38	4.32	4.38	0.4	89.1	51	10.5	43.3

Zach Duke, continued

Pitch Shape vs LHH

Pitch Shape vs RHH

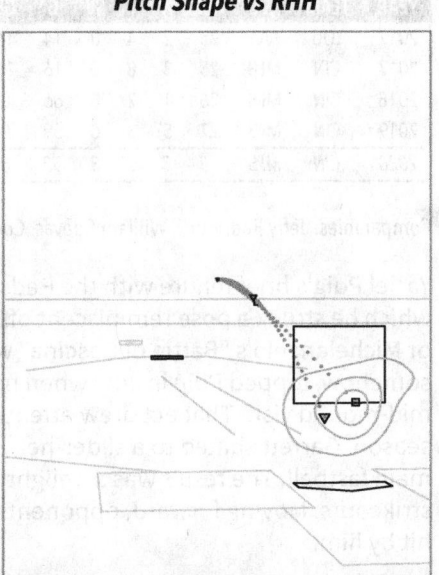

Type	Frequency	Velocity	H Movement	V Movement
● Fastball	7.5%	88.4 [88]	3.2 [116]	-23.8 [79]
☐ Sinker	48.6%	89.4 [83]	12.4 [102]	-28.6 [71]
+ Cutter				
▲ Changeup				
✕ Splitter				
▽ Slider	32.4%	80.6 [84]	-8.9 [116]	-34.5 [96]
◇ Curveball	11.3%	74.4 [86]	-12.5 [120]	-51.8 [91]
⊕ Slow Curveball				
✱ Knuckleball				
▼ Screwball				

Reds Player Analysis - 53

Amir Garrett LHP

Born: 05/03/92 Age: 28 Bats: R Throws: L
Height: 6'5" Weight: 228 Origin: Round 22, 2011 Draft (#685 overall)

YEAR	TEAM	LVL	AGE	W	L	SV	G	GS	IP	H	HR	BB/9	K/9	K	GB%	BABIP
2017	LOU	AAA	25	2	4	0	14	14	67^2	79	7	3.2	8.1	61	41%	.346
2017	CIN	MLB	25	3	8	0	16	14	70^2	74	23	5.1	8.0	63	44%	.264
2018	CIN	MLB	26	1	2	0	66	0	63	56	8	3.6	10.1	71	39%	.306
2019	CIN	MLB	27	5	3	0	69	0	56	44	7	5.6	12.5	78	55%	.303
2020	CIN	MLB	28	3	3	3	52	0	55	50	8	4.9	12.0	74	51%	.324

Comparables: Jefry Rodriguez, William Cuevas, Cody Reed

Yasiel Puig's brief tenure with the Reds included a brawl with the Pirates during which he struck a pose reminiscent of Tintoretto's "Massacre of the Innocents" or Michelangelo's "Battle of Cascina" while battling the entire roster. Garrett, somehow, topped Puig in July when he charged the Pirates dugout by himself mid-mound visit. That act drew attention away from an otherwise excellent season. Garrett shifted to a slider-heavy approach and made the two-seamer his main fastball. The result was a delightful combination of grounders and strikeouts. Moving forward, opponents won't want to hit against him or, um, be hit by him.

YEAR	TEAM	LVL	AGE	WHIP	ERA	DRA	WARP	MPH	FB%	WHF	CSP
2017	LOU	AAA	25	1.52	5.72	5.69	0.0				
2017	CIN	MLB	25	1.61	7.39	7.46	-1.5	94.9	62.1	9.1	47.7
2018	CIN	MLB	26	1.29	4.29	4.41	0.4	97.6	63.1	14.8	47.5
2019	CIN	MLB	27	1.41	3.21	3.35	1.2	97.5	42	17	42
2020	CIN	MLB	28	1.45	4.43	4.34	0.7	96.2	55.1	14	45.5

Amir Garrett, continued

Pitch Shape vs LHH   Pitch Shape vs RHH

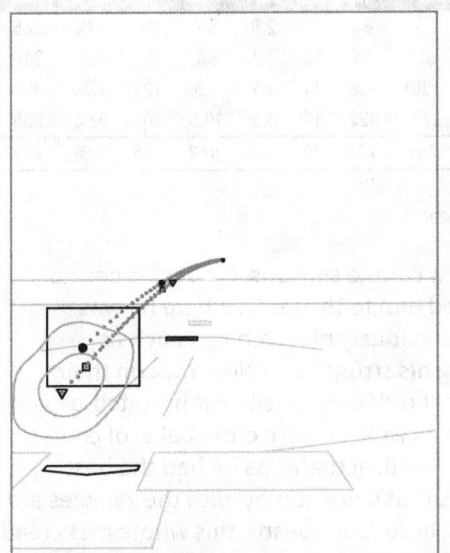 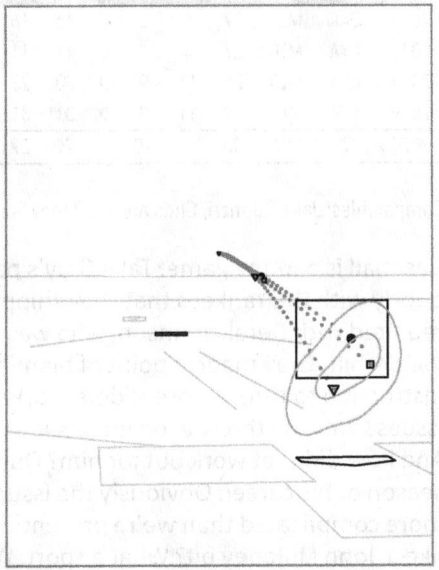

Type	Frequency	Velocity	H Movement	V Movement
● Fastball	11.9%	96 [110]	11.6 [79]	-15.7 [101]
☐ Sinker	30.1%	95.5 [115]	13.3 [96]	-18.3 [107]
+ Cutter				
▲ Changeup				
✕ Splitter				
▽ Slider	58.0%	86.1 [107]	-0.3 [80]	-30 [109]
◇ Curveball				
✥ Slow Curveball				
✱ Knuckleball				
▼ Screwball				

Sonny Gray RHP
Born: 11/07/89 Age: 30 Bats: R Throws: R
Height: 5'10" Weight: 192 Origin: Round 1, 2011 Draft (#18 overall)

YEAR	TEAM	LVL	AGE	W	L	SV	G	GS	IP	H	HR	BB/9	K/9	K	GB%	BABIP
2017	OAK	MLB	27	6	5	0	16	16	97	84	8	2.8	8.7	94	58%	.285
2017	NYA	MLB	27	4	7	0	11	11	65^1	55	11	3.7	8.1	59	48%	.246
2018	NYA	MLB	28	11	9	0	30	23	130^1	138	14	3.9	8.5	123	52%	.326
2019	CIN	MLB	29	11	8	0	31	31	175^1	122	17	3.5	10.5	205	53%	.255
2020	CIN	MLB	30	10	10	0	29	29	163	144	20	3.7	10.2	185	52%	.297

Comparables: Jake Odorizzi, Chris Archer, Danny Salazar

Baseball is a funny game. Take Gray's past couple seasons. He performed so poorly with the Yankees that they shipped him to the Reds, where he was reunited with Derek Johnson, who was previously his pitching coach at Vanderbilt. Gray made a point of blaming his struggles in New York on their instruction to throw more sliders. So, what did he do to correct his pitch-usage issues? Why, he threw even more sliders, as well as more curveballs, of course. And how did that work out for him? Quite well, actually, as he had the best season of his career. Obviously the issues that were at play with the Yankees are more complicated than we're presenting here. But doesn't this whole mess read like a John Mulaney bit? What a sport. What. A. Sport.

YEAR	TEAM	LVL	AGE	WHIP	ERA	DRA	WARP	MPH	FB%	WHF	CSP
2017	OAK	MLB	27	1.18	3.43	4.22	1.5	95.3	63.7	13.1	45.5
2017	NYA	MLB	27	1.26	3.72	4.04	1.1	95.0	63.7	12	41.8
2018	NYA	MLB	28	1.50	4.90	5.00	0.4	95.4	57.2	10.8	45.2
2019	CIN	MLB	29	1.08	2.87	2.98	5.3	95.2	50.5	11.7	42.8
2020	CIN	MLB	30	1.29	3.70	3.77	3.7	94.5	55.6	11.7	43.7

Sonny Gray, continued

Pitch Shape vs LHH
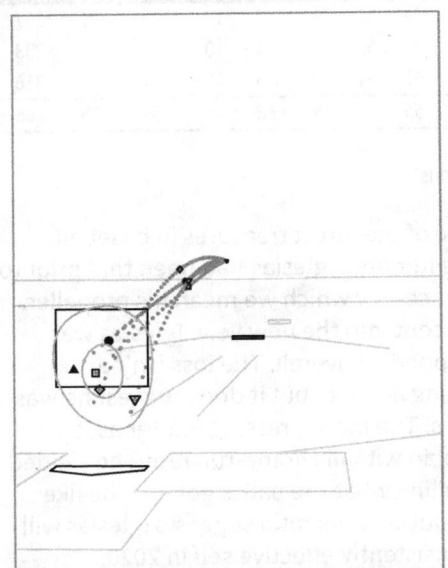

Pitch Shape vs RHH
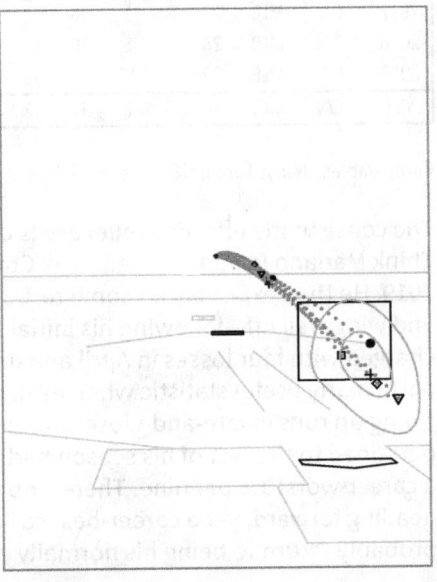

Type	Frequency	Velocity	H Movement	V Movement
● Fastball	27.8%	93.7 [104]	-1.4 [124]	-14.2 [105]
☐ Sinker	21.2%	93.2 [103]	-10.2 [116]	-19.2 [104]
✚ Cutter				
▲ Changeup	3.0%	89.8 [117]	-10.8 [102]	-22 [116]
✕ Splitter				
▽ Slider	20.5%	84.9 [102]	14.3 [139]	-37.9 [86]
◇ Curveball	25.7%	82.2 [112]	14.6 [129]	-47.5 [100]
✦ Slow Curveball				
✱ Knuckleball				
▼ Screwball				

Reds Player Analysis - 57

Raisel Iglesias   RHP
Born: 01/04/90   Age: 30   Bats: R   Throws: R
Height: 6'2"   Weight: 188   Origin: International Free Agent, 2014

YEAR	TEAM	LVL	AGE	W	L	SV	G	GS	IP	H	HR	BB/9	K/9	K	GB%	BABIP
2017	CIN	MLB	27	3	3	28	63	0	76	57	5	3.2	10.9	92	43%	.287
2018	CIN	MLB	28	2	5	30	66	0	72	52	12	3.1	10.0	80	40%	.233
2019	CIN	MLB	29	3	12	34	68	0	67	61	12	2.8	12.0	89	31%	.316
2020	CIN	MLB	30	3	2	30	52	0	55	45	8	3.3	11.2	69	37%	.286

Comparables: Jeurys Familia, Erik Goeddel, Héctor Neris

The consistently effective relief ace is one of the rarest treasures in baseball. Think Mariano Rivera, or even peak Craig Kimbrel. Iglesias had been that prior to 2019. He then experienced some turbulence—by which we mean his propeller and wings fell off—following his initial ascent into the new year. Iglesias was charged with four losses in April and dropped 12 overall. The loss isn't a particularly useful statistic when evaluating anyone, but it does suggest he was giving up runs in late-and-close situations. The more pressing matter as it pertained to the rest of his season had to do with his home-run rate—he yielded a career-worst 1.6 per nine. There's no telling what the ball is going to be like heading forward, yet a career-best strikeout-to-walk ratio suggests Iglesias will probably return to being his normally consistently effective self in 2020.

YEAR	TEAM	LVL	AGE	WHIP	ERA	DRA	WARP	MPH	FB%	WHF	CSP
2017	CIN	MLB	27	1.11	2.49	3.34	1.6	99.1	57.1	15.1	50.2
2018	CIN	MLB	28	1.07	2.38	3.48	1.2	98.3	50.2	16.5	47.9
2019	CIN	MLB	29	1.22	4.16	3.82	1.1	97.9	47.8	16.6	46.1
2020	CIN	MLB	30	1.19	3.40	3.55	1.1	97.6	50.9	16.1	47.6

Raisel Iglesias, continued

Pitch Shape vs LHH

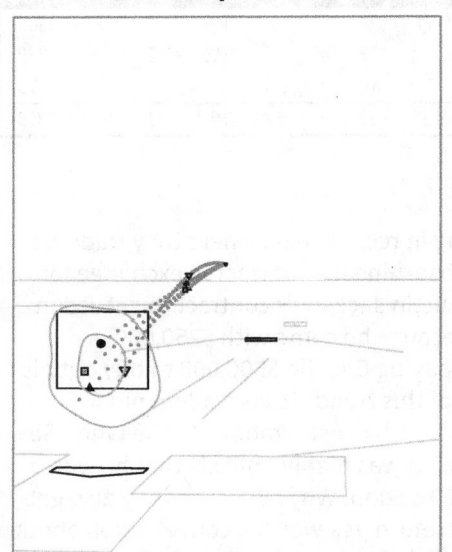

Pitch Shape vs RHH

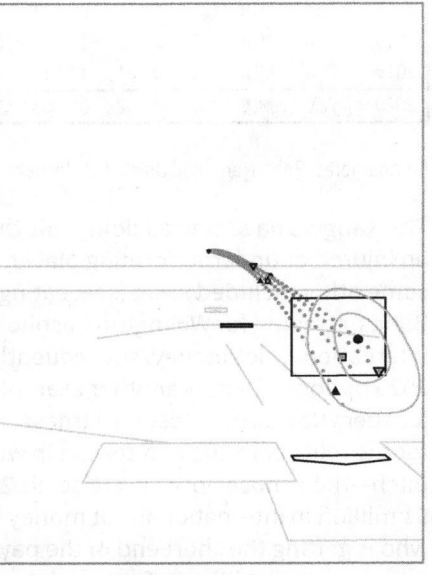

Type		Frequency	Velocity	H Movement	V Movement
●	Fastball	40.2%	95.7 [109]	-6.9 [100]	-13.3 [107]
□	Sinker	7.6%	95.3 [114]	-13.5 [95]	-17.8 [109]
+	Cutter				
▲	Changeup	21.7%	89.3 [114]	-13.9 [87]	-27.7 [99]
×	Splitter				
▽	Slider	30.5%	84.2 [99]	9.7 [120]	-32.8 [101]
◇	Curveball				
⊕	Slow Curveball				
✱	Knuckleball				
▼	Screwball				

Reds Player Analysis - 59

Cincinnati Reds 2020

Nate Jones   RHP
Born: 01/28/86   Age: 34   Bats: R   Throws: R
Height: 6'5"   Weight: 220   Origin: Round 5, 2007 Draft (#179 overall)

YEAR	TEAM	LVL	AGE	W	L	SV	G	GS	IP	H	HR	BB/9	K/9	K	GB%	BABIP
2017	CHA	MLB	31	1	0	0	11	0	11²	9	1	4.6	11.6	15	59%	.308
2018	CHA	MLB	32	2	2	5	33	0	30	28	4	4.5	9.6	32	41%	.289
2019	CHA	MLB	33	0	1	1	13	0	10¹	10	2	6.1	8.7	10	52%	.296
2020	TEX	MLB	34	2	2	0	33	0	35	32	5	3.7	10.4	41	44%	.306

Comparables: Robb Nen, Brad Brach, Pat Neshek

The Rangers have started doing this thing in recent years where they trade for an injured or underperforming player, absorbing his contract in exchange for some other included asset (see: eating Austin Jackson's contract to get Jason Bahr, or trading for Welington Castillo because he came with $250,000 in international slot money, subsequently paying Castillo $500,000 to buy out his 2020 option). Jones is another example of this trend. Texas traded minor leaguers Ray Castro, Joseph Jarneski and cash considerations to the White Sox for the reliever in 2019—a season in which it was highly unlikely that he would pitch—then chose not to exercise his 2020 option. Why? Because they also got $1 million in international slot money in return. It's worth a conversation about who is getting the short end of the paycheck if teams are willing to part with prospects and millions of actual dollars just to be allowed a larger pool of money that they can spend on Latin American players. One read would be that—since teams are paying X amount of additional dollars anyway—the market is telling us that those Latin American players are worth more money and the cap is artificially depressing their ability to earn a fair paycheck. Anyway, Nate Jones didn't throw a single pitch in a game at any level as a member of the Texas Rangers; yay capitalism!

YEAR	TEAM	LVL	AGE	WHIP	ERA	DRA	WARP	MPH	FB%	WHF	CSP
2017	CHA	MLB	31	1.29	2.31	4.95	0.0	98.9	52.5	13	41.5
2018	CHA	MLB	32	1.43	3.00	4.55	0.1	99.0	64.7	15.2	47.1
2019	CHA	MLB	33	1.65	3.48	5.37	0.0	96.8	58.3	10.2	46.3
2020	TEX	MLB	34	1.33	4.35	4.38	0.3	97.3	60	13.2	44.7

Nate Jones, continued

Pitch Shape vs LHH

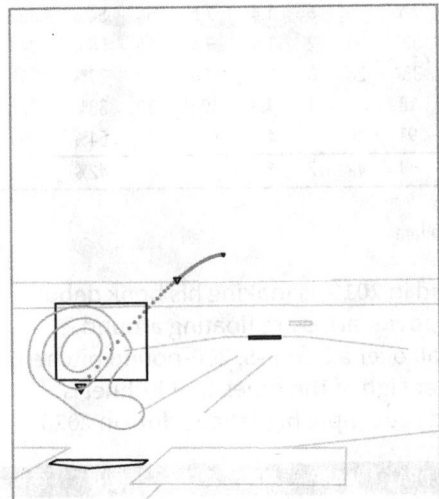

Pitch Shape vs RHH

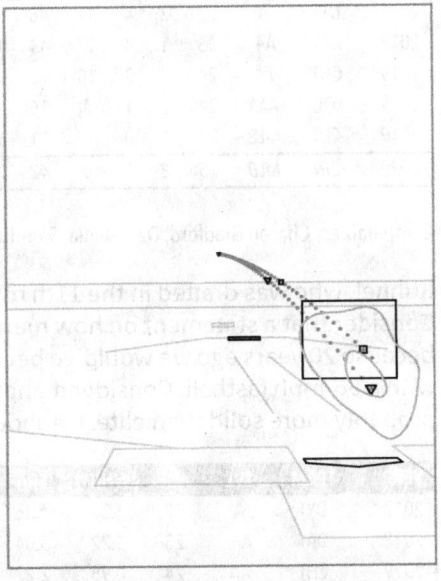

Type	Frequency	Velocity	H Movement	V Movement
● Fastball				
□ Sinker	58.3%	95.6 [115]	-11.5 [107]	-12.8 [127]
+ Cutter				
▲ Changeup				
✕ Splitter				
▽ Slider	38.8%	87.7 [114]	0.5 [81]	-26.7 [118]
◇ Curveball				
⊕ Slow Curveball				
✳ Knuckleball				
▼ Screwball				

Joel Kuhnel RHP

Born: 02/19/95 Age: 25 Bats: R Throws: R
Height: 6'5" Weight: 260 Origin: Round 11, 2016 Draft (#318 overall)

YEAR	TEAM	LVL	AGE	W	L	SV	G	GS	IP	H	HR	BB/9	K/9	K	GB%	BABIP
2017	DYT	A	22	2	4	11	48	0	64	78	6	1.4	7.6	54	54%	.353
2018	DAY	A+	23	1	4	17	44	0	53^1	54	2	1.9	9.4	56	54%	.340
2019	CHT	AA	24	3	2	10	25	0	35^2	26	5	2.0	7.6	30	39%	.212
2019	LOU	AAA	24	2	1	4	16	0	18	13	1	4.0	10.0	20	38%	.273
2019	CIN	MLB	24	1	0	0	11	0	9^2	8	1	4.7	8.4	9	54%	.259
2020	CIN	MLB	25	2	2	0	42	0	44	42	7	3.8	9.9	49	42%	.303

Comparables: Chasen Bradford, Dan Slania, Sam Tuivailala

Kuhnel, who was drafted in the 11th round in 2016, is making his book debut. Consider that a statement on how many power arms are floating around, because 20 years ago we would've been all over a 6-foot-5, 260-pound pitcher with a 96-mph fastball. Consider it another sign of the times that Kuhnel is probably more solid than elite. He should see ample big-league duty in 2020.

YEAR	TEAM	LVL	AGE	WHIP	ERA	DRA	WARP	MPH	FB%	WHF	CSP
2017	DYT	A	22	1.38	4.36	5.10	-0.1				
2018	DAY	A+	23	1.22	3.04	3.84	0.7				
2019	CHT	AA	24	0.95	2.27	3.23	0.6				
2019	LOU	AAA	24	1.17	2.00	3.41	0.5				
2019	CIN	MLB	24	1.34	4.66	4.37	0.1	98.4	61.5	14.5	42.7
2020	CIN	MLB	25	1.38	4.33	4.36	0.5	98.1	62.9	14.8	43.7

Joel Kuhnel, continued

Pitch Shape vs LHH	Pitch Shape vs RHH
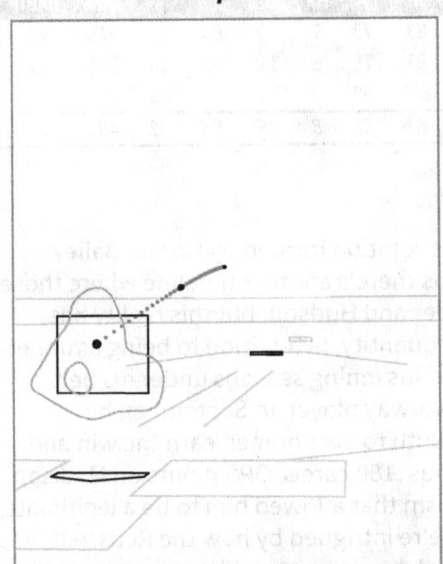	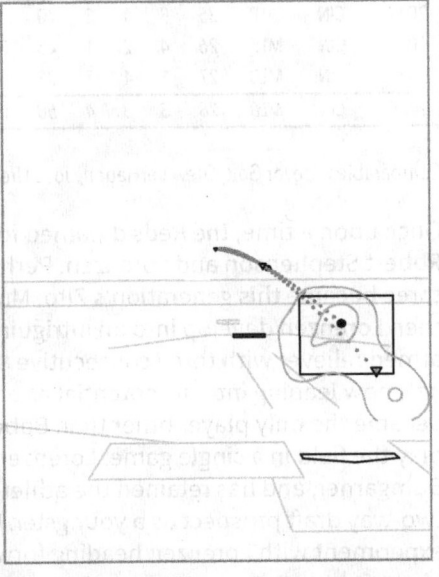

Type	Frequency	Velocity	H Movement	V Movement
● Fastball	43.4%	96.2 [111]	-7.4 [98]	-13.5 [106]
◻ Sinker	18.1%	95.9 [117]	-13.3 [96]	-16.9 [112]
+ Cutter				
▲ Changeup	6.0%	89.5 [115]	-9 [110]	-26.5 [103]
✕ Splitter				
▽ Slider	32.5%	86.1 [107]	3.5 [94]	-32.1 [103]
◇ Curveball				
⊕ Slow Curveball				
✱ Knuckleball				
▼ Screwball				

Michael Lorenzen RHP

Born: 01/04/92 Age: 28 Bats: R Throws: R
Height: 6'3" Weight: 217 Origin: Round 1, 2013 Draft (#38 overall)

YEAR	TEAM	LVL	AGE	W	L	SV	G	GS	IP	H	HR	BB/9	K/9	K	GB%	BABIP
2017	CIN	MLB	25	8	4	2	70	0	83	78	9	3.7	8.7	80	57%	.295
2018	CIN	MLB	26	4	2	1	45	3	81	78	6	3.8	6.0	54	52%	.291
2019	CIN	MLB	27	1	4	7	73	0	83^1	68	9	3.0	9.2	85	46%	.269
2020	CIN	MLB	28	3	3	4	58	0	61	58	8	3.9	9.1	62	48%	.301

Comparables: Trevor Gott, Drew VerHagen, José Ureña

Once upon a time, the Reds dreamed for a rotation fronted by Homer Bailey, Robert Stephenson and Lorenzen. Perhaps there's another timeline where those three became this generation's Zito, Mulder and Hudson, but this reality has seen Lorenzen develop into an intriguing quantity. In addition to being a rubber-armed reliever with three consecutive 80-plus inning seasons under his belt, he's now leaning into his potential as a two-way player. In September, he became the only player other than Babe Ruth to ever homer, earn the win and play the field in a single game. Lorenzen has .180 career OPS points on Madison Bumgarner, and has retained the athleticism that allowed him to be a legitimate two-way draft prospect as a youngster. We're intrigued by how the Reds will experiment with Lorenzen heading forward, because it could come to serve as a blueprint.

YEAR	TEAM	LVL	AGE	WHIP	ERA	DRA	WARP	MPH	FB%	WHF	CSP
2017	CIN	MLB	25	1.35	4.45	4.37	0.7	98.2	51.3	11.3	47.8
2018	CIN	MLB	26	1.38	3.11	5.87	-0.8	97.3	51.5	7.6	48.6
2019	CIN	MLB	27	1.15	2.92	3.78	1.4	98.3	36.1	15.2	44.2
2020	CIN	MLB	28	1.37	4.15	4.16	0.8	97.4	45.4	11.8	46.8

Michael Lorenzen, continued

Pitch Shape vs LHH

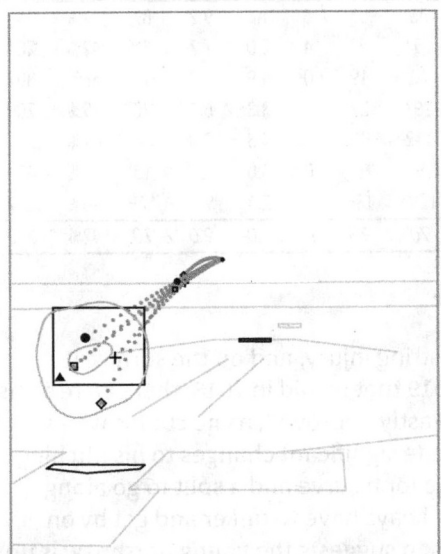

Pitch Shape vs RHH

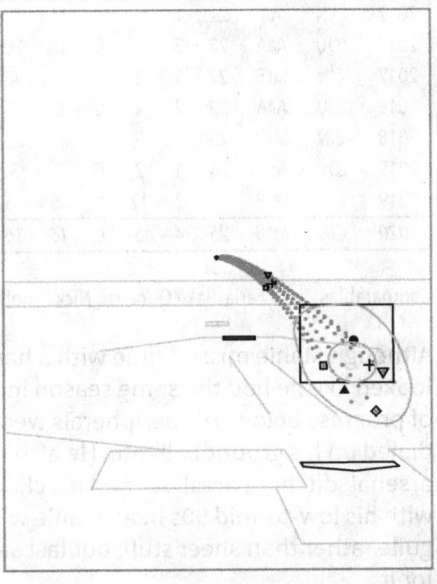

Type	Frequency	Velocity	H Movement	V Movement
● Fastball	21.3%	97.3 [114]	-9.3 [89]	-11.4 [112]
☐ Sinker	14.8%	96.6 [121]	-13 [98]	-15.7 [117]
+ Cutter	27.8%	94 [133]	-0.9 [84]	-18.6 [120]
▲ Changeup	19.5%	87.5 [108]	-13.3 [90]	-23.7 [111]
✕ Splitter				
▽ Slider	10.0%	86.8 [110]	5.1 [100]	-31.7 [104]
◇ Curveball	6.5%	83.8 [117]	2.9 [81]	-44.5 [107]
⊕ Slow Curveball				
✱ Knuckleball				
▼ Screwball				

Cincinnati Reds 2020

Tyler Mahle   RHP
Born: 09/29/94   Age: 25   Bats: R   Throws: R
Height: 6'3"   Weight: 210   Origin: Round 7, 2013 Draft (#225 overall)

YEAR	TEAM	LVL	AGE	W	L	SV	G	GS	IP	H	HR	BB/9	K/9	K	GB%	BABIP
2017	PEN	AA	22	7	3	0	14	14	85	57	5	1.8	9.2	87	42%	.245
2017	LOU	AAA	22	3	4	0	10	10	59^1	52	4	2.0	7.7	51	42%	.281
2017	CIN	MLB	22	1	2	0	4	4	20	19	0	4.9	6.3	14	56%	.302
2018	LOU	AAA	23	2	1	0	5	5	29^2	22	4	3.3	6.1	20	39%	.209
2018	CIN	MLB	23	7	9	0	23	23	112	125	22	4.3	8.8	110	41%	.324
2019	LOU	AAA	24	1	2	0	3	3	9	8	0	3.0	13.0	13	65%	.400
2019	CIN	MLB	24	3	12	0	25	25	129^2	136	25	2.4	9.0	129	48%	.307
2020	CIN	MLB	25	4	5	0	16	16	70	72	11	3.0	9.0	70	47%	.312

Comparables: Jake Faria, Jake Odorizzi, Nick Kingham

Although Mahle missed time with a hamstring injury, and on the surface it looked like he had the same season in 2019 that he did in 2018, there were signs of progress below. His peripherals were vastly improved, as he cut his walks and dialed up his groundball rate. He also made significant changes to his pitching arsenal, ditching his slider and his change for a curve and a split to go along with his low-to-mid 90s heat. Mahle will always have to tinker and get by on guile rather than sheer stuff, but last season suggests the young northpaw is up for it.

YEAR	TEAM	LVL	AGE	WHIP	ERA	DRA	WARP	MPH	FB%	WHF	CSP
2017	PEN	AA	22	0.87	1.59	2.65	2.6				
2017	LOU	AAA	22	1.10	2.73	3.25	1.6				
2017	CIN	MLB	22	1.50	2.70	5.48	0.0	95.9	65.8	7.9	47.2
2018	LOU	AAA	23	1.11	2.73	3.89	0.6				
2018	CIN	MLB	23	1.59	4.98	6.30	-1.3	96.0	67.8	11.4	49.6
2019	LOU	AAA	24	1.22	4.00	3.37	0.3				
2019	CIN	MLB	24	1.31	5.14	4.82	1.3	96.1	56.7	10.7	49.3
2020	CIN	MLB	25	1.37	4.52	4.54	1.0	95.8	63.3	11.1	50.1

Tyler Mahle, continued

Pitch Shape vs LHH	Pitch Shape vs RHH
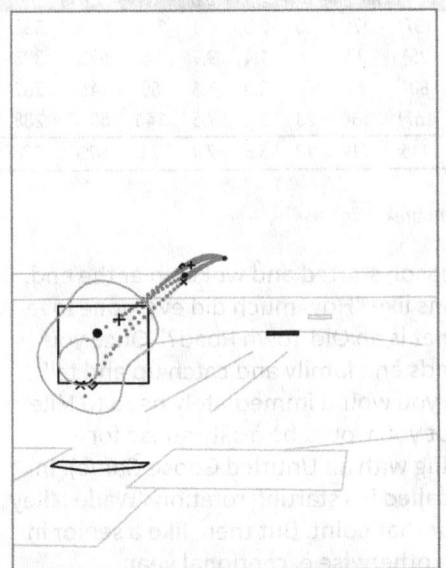	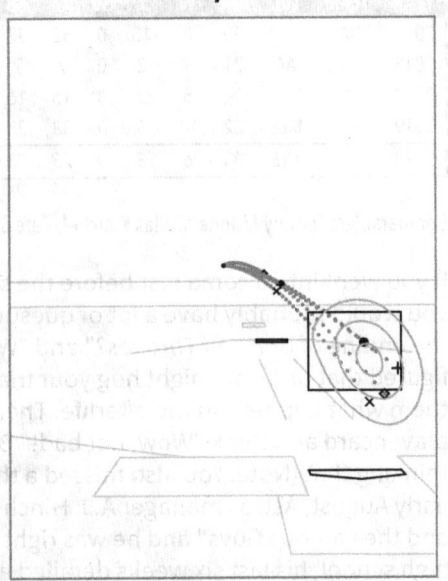

Type	Frequency	Velocity	H Movement	V Movement
● Fastball	56.7%	93.7 [104]	-10 [86]	-15.4 [101]
☐ Sinker				
+ Cutter	6.6%	90.4 [111]	0.7 [93]	-20.9 [112]
▲ Changeup				
✕ Splitter	13.5%	87.5 [111]	-9.2 [95]	-27.9 [104]
▽ Slider				
◇ Curveball	22.7%	80.7 [107]	7 [98]	-43.8 [108]
⊕ Slow Curveball				
✱ Knuckleball				
▼ Screwball				

Wade Miley LHP

Born: 11/13/86 Age: 33 Bats: L Throws: L
Height: 6'0" Weight: 220 Origin: Round 1, 2008 Draft (#43 overall)

YEAR	TEAM	LVL	AGE	W	L	SV	G	GS	IP	H	HR	BB/9	K/9	K	GB%	BABIP
2017	BAL	MLB	30	8	15	0	32	32	157¹	179	25	5.3	8.1	142	51%	.332
2018	BLX	AA	31	1	2	0	7	7	25¹	27	3	1.4	9.9	28	59%	.393
2018	MIL	MLB	31	5	2	0	16	16	80²	71	3	3.0	5.6	50	54%	.269
2019	HOU	MLB	32	14	6	0	33	33	167¹	164	23	3.3	7.5	140	50%	.288
2020	CIN	MLB	33	6	8	0	23	23	116	119	17	3.5	7.4	95	50%	.298

Comparables: Tommy Milone, Dallas Keuchel, Pete Schourek

If you went into a coma just before the season started and woke up at the end, you would probably have a lot of questions like "How much did everyone love the ending of *Game of Thrones*?" and "What is an Old Town Road?" Once you figured that out, you might hug your friends and family and catch up and tell them what happens in the afterlife. Then you would immediately head to Miley's player card and think "Wow, not bad!" But you would be a silly goose for thinking that (Note: You also missed a thing with an Untitled Goose Game). In early August, Astros manager A.J. Hinch called his starting rotation "Wade Miley and the Famous Guys" and he was right at that point. But then, like a senior in high school, his last six weeks derailed an otherwise exceptional year.

YEAR	TEAM	LVL	AGE	WHIP	ERA	DRA	WARP	MPH	FB%	WHF	CSP
2017	BAL	MLB	30	1.73	5.61	7.20	-2.9	93.7	53.4	9	36.9
2018	BLX	AA	31	1.22	3.55	4.87	0.1				
2018	MIL	MLB	31	1.21	2.57	4.13	1.1	93.0	20	9.9	42.5
2019	HOU	MLB	32	1.34	3.98	5.42	0.6	92.3	21.9	10.4	42.4
2020	CIN	MLB	33	1.42	4.61	4.60	1.6	91.8	31.2	9.7	40.6

Wade Miley, continued

Pitch Shape vs LHH

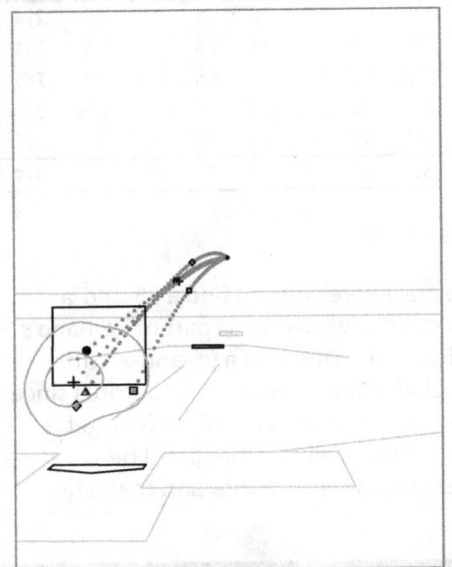

Pitch Shape vs RHH

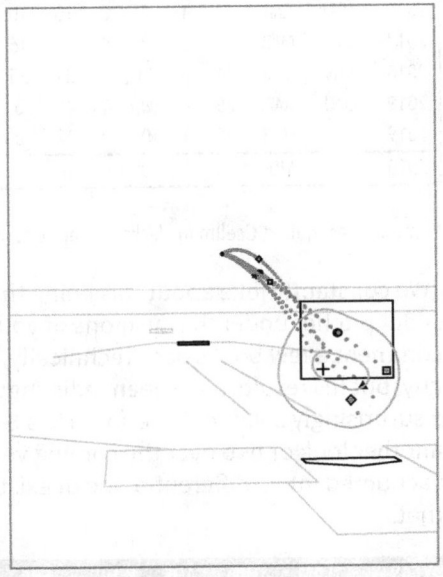

Type	Frequency	Velocity	H Movement	V Movement
● Fastball	15.9%	91.1 [96]	3.8 [114]	-14.4 [104]
□ Sinker	6.0%	89.6 [85]	10.7 [112]	-17.5 [110]
+ Cutter	47.1%	87.5 [93]	-1.9 [100]	-24.9 [97]
▲ Changeup	20.7%	81.4 [86]	13.5 [89]	-27.8 [99]
✕ Splitter				
▽ Slider				
◇ Curveball	9.2%	75.7 [90]	-6 [94]	-53.7 [87]
⊕ Slow Curveball				
✱ Knuckleball				
▼ Screwball				

Sal Romano   RHP

Born: 10/12/93   Age: 26   Bats: L   Throws: R
Height: 6'5"   Weight: 255   Origin: Round 23, 2011 Draft (#715 overall)

YEAR	TEAM	LVL	AGE	W	L	SV	G	GS	IP	H	HR	BB/9	K/9	K	GB%	BABIP
2017	LOU	AAA	23	1	4	0	10	10	49^1	49	1	3.1	5.8	32	50%	.298
2017	CIN	MLB	23	5	8	0	16	16	87	91	9	3.8	7.6	73	53%	.314
2018	CIN	MLB	24	8	11	0	39	25	145^2	155	23	3.3	6.5	105	47%	.288
2019	LOU	AAA	25	4	8	1	43	5	69^1	72	6	3.4	9.9	76	47%	.349
2019	CIN	MLB	25	1	0	2	12	0	16^1	22	4	4.4	8.8	16	38%	.375
2020	CIN	MLB	26	3	3	0	40	3	55	62	9	3.4	7.2	44	46%	.314

Comparables: Robert Gsellman, Jackson Stephens, Nate Adcock

"We constantly joke about this being the era where you can find a 95-and-a-slider pitcher under the cushions of your couch," we wrote as part of Romano's comment a few books ago. Technically, Romano is more of a 96-and-a-cutter guy, but his results have been indistinguishable from generic sofa detritus since a surprisingly solid rookie effort. He's 6-foot-5 and throws hard, so he'll get another look or two over the coming years. Eventually, Romano will be vacuumed into a different plane of existence—same as us all—and that'll be that.

YEAR	TEAM	LVL	AGE	WHIP	ERA	DRA	WARP	MPH	FB%	WHF	CSP
2017	LOU	AAA	23	1.34	3.47	4.73	0.5				
2017	CIN	MLB	23	1.47	4.45	4.55	1.0	97.6	62.7	9.6	46.6
2018	CIN	MLB	24	1.43	5.31	5.76	-0.8	96.4	65.6	8.6	49.1
2019	LOU	AAA	25	1.41	4.28	4.84	1.0				
2019	CIN	MLB	25	1.84	7.71	6.07	-0.1	97.4	64.2	7.5	48.7
2020	CIN	MLB	26	1.51	5.40	5.29	0.2	96.4	65.8	9	49.2

Sal Romano, continued

Pitch Shape vs LHH

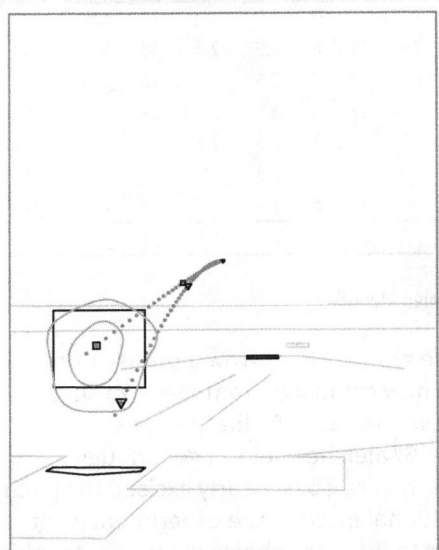

Pitch Shape vs RHH

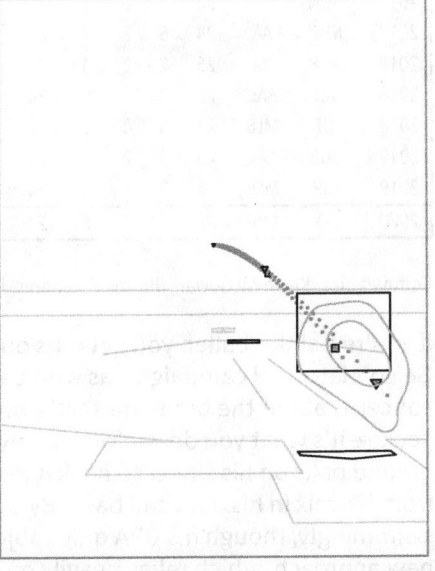

Type	Frequency	Velocity	H Movement	V Movement
● Fastball	7.8%	96.4 [111]	-8.6 [92]	-13 [108]
☐ Sinker	56.3%	95.9 [117]	-11.6 [106]	-15.3 [118]
+ Cutter				
▲ Changeup				
✕ Splitter				
▽ Slider	35.8%	86.8 [110]	3.4 [93]	-33.7 [98]
◇ Curveball				
✤ Slow Curveball				
✱ Knuckleball				
▼ Screwball				

Cincinnati Reds 2020

Justin Shafer RHP

Born: 09/18/92 Age: 27 Bats: R Throws: R
Height: 6'2" Weight: 195 Origin: Round 8, 2014 Draft (#234 overall)

YEAR	TEAM	LVL	AGE	W	L	SV	G	GS	IP	H	HR	BB/9	K/9	K	GB%	BABIP
2017	DUN	A+	24	0	0	0	5	0	9.1	7	0	1.9	12.5	13	62%	.333
2017	NHP	AA	24	5	2	1	37	0	58	45	6	4.0	7.4	48	51%	.244
2018	NHP	AA	25	2	2	1	13	0	17.1	12	1	2.6	8.8	17	58%	.262
2018	BUF	AAA	25	3	3	15	34	0	38.1	27	0	3.8	7.5	32	45%	.252
2018	TOR	MLB	25	0	0	0	6	0	8.1	6	1	7.6	2.2	2	45%	.179
2019	BUF	AAA	26	0	2	7	24	0	30.2	29	3	2.3	10.3	35	34%	.317
2019	TOR	MLB	26	2	1	1	34	0	39.2	41	6	5.7	8.8	39	32%	.315
2020	CIN	MLB	27	1	1	0	21	0	22	22	4	4.3	8.5	21	36%	.294

Comparables: Kevin McGowan, Jimmy Yacabonis, Damien Magnifico

if you're a sinkerballer, you get outs on the ground. To borrow a phrase from Geico's latest ad campaign—as with each new campaign from them, raising concerns about the brand mascot's whereabouts and the lifespan of a gecko—it's what you do. Unfortunately for Shafer, he couldn't get enough ground balls on his sinker to hack it in the majors, so he nearly excised the pitch from his mix in his Jays call back. By traditional metrics, the experiment went swimmingly, though his DRA quite objects to the word choice there. Whether his new approach, which relies heavily on his four-seamer and a new cutter, sticks in 2020 with Derek Johnson now in his ear really just depends on how much all involved believe in Santa Claus.

YEAR	TEAM	LVL	AGE	WHIP	ERA	DRA	WARP	MPH	FB%	WHF	CSP
2017	DUN	A+	24	0.96	0.00	3.53	0.1				
2017	NHP	AA	24	1.22	3.41	3.32	1.0				
2018	NHP	AA	25	0.98	0.52	2.99	0.4				
2018	BUF	AAA	25	1.12	1.41	3.58	0.7				
2018	TOR	MLB	25	1.56	3.24	7.96	-0.3	94.6	68.5	7.5	43.3
2019	BUF	AAA	26	1.21	3.52	3.36	0.8				
2019	TOR	MLB	26	1.66	3.86	7.46	-0.9	95.8	51.6	12.6	44.6
2020	CIN	MLB	27	1.49	5.17	5.08	0.1	95.1	54.6	12	44.5

Justin Shafer, continued

Pitch Shape vs LHH

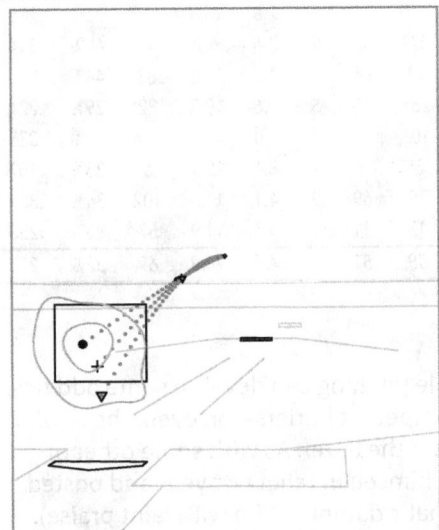

Pitch Shape vs RHH

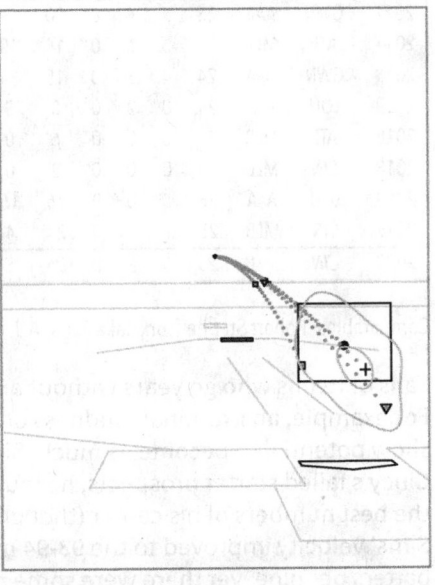

Type	Frequency	Velocity	H Movement	V Movement
● Fastball	44.7%	94.8 [107]	-5.5 [106]	-11.8 [111]
□ Sinker	7.0%	93.7 [105]	-13.2 [96]	-18.3 [107]
+ Cutter	19.4%	90.5 [111]	1.8 [100]	-22 [108]
▲ Changeup	3.4%	87.7 [109]	-11.4 [99]	-25 [107]
✕ Splitter				
▽ Slider	25.5%	85.9 [107]	5.9 [104]	-32.5 [102]
◇ Curveball				
✦ Slow Curveball				
✱ Knuckleball				
▼ Screwball				

Lucas Sims RHP
Born: 05/10/94   Age: 26   Bats: R   Throws: R
Height: 6'2"   Weight: 225   Origin: Round 1, 2012 Draft (#21 overall)

YEAR	TEAM	LVL	AGE	W	L	SV	G	GS	IP	H	HR	BB/9	K/9	K	GB%	BABIP
2017	GWN	AAA	23	7	4	0	20	19	115^1	95	19	2.8	10.3	132	35%	.275
2017	ATL	MLB	23	3	6	0	14	10	57^2	64	9	3.6	6.9	44	40%	.314
2018	GWN	AAA	24	4	3	0	15	14	73	66	6	4.2	10.2	83	44%	.330
2018	LOU	AAA	24	0	2	0	5	5	28^1	20	5	1.6	10.2	32	29%	.224
2018	ATL	MLB	24	0	0	0	6	0	10^1	12	2	7.0	8.7	10	42%	.323
2018	CIN	MLB	24	0	0	0	3	0	5^1	3	1	8.4	10.1	6	23%	.167
2019	LOU	AAA	25	5	0	0	16	16	79	69	9	4.1	11.6	102	34%	.321
2019	CIN	MLB	25	2	1	0	24	4	43	31	8	4.0	11.9	57	26%	.253
2020	CIN	MLB	26	3	3	0	36	5	58	51	10	4.2	10.8	69	32%	.292

Comparables: Robert Stephenson, Jake Faria, A.J. Cole

Fans of teams who go years without ample pitching can develop some odd tics. For example, an irrational fondness of competent hurlers—or, even, those who show potential to become as much. Sims is the latter. As with some other of Cincy's failed starter prospects, he found himself in relief last year and posted the best numbers of his career (though that's damning him with faint praise). Sims' velocity improved to the 93-94 mph range and he struck out nearly 12 batters per nine, yet there were some red flags worth acknowledging—namely, that his command remained poor and his extreme flyball tendencies didn't play nice with the rabbit ball. There's some potential value here is as a multi-inning reliever—perhaps a hair more if the hare ball goes away—but let's not get too overzealous about what he is or what he's likely to become.

YEAR	TEAM	LVL	AGE	WHIP	ERA	DRA	WARP	MPH	FB%	WHF	CSP
2017	GWN	AAA	23	1.14	3.75	3.81	2.4				
2017	ATL	MLB	23	1.51	5.62	6.13	-0.4	94.4	46.5	9	46.7
2018	GWN	AAA	24	1.37	2.84	4.53	0.8				
2018	LOU	AAA	24	0.88	3.81	5.48	0.0				
2018	ATL	MLB	24	1.94	7.84	6.38	-0.2	95.1	55.7	10	37.4
2018	CIN	MLB	24	1.50	6.75	3.59	0.1	94.3	55	15.3	49.3
2019	LOU	AAA	25	1.33	4.56	3.48	2.5				
2019	CIN	MLB	25	1.16	4.60	4.30	0.6	95.2	50.6	16	40.9
2020	CIN	MLB	26	1.35	4.44	4.44	0.7	94.5	50.7	13	43.3

Lucas Sims, continued

Pitch Shape vs LHH

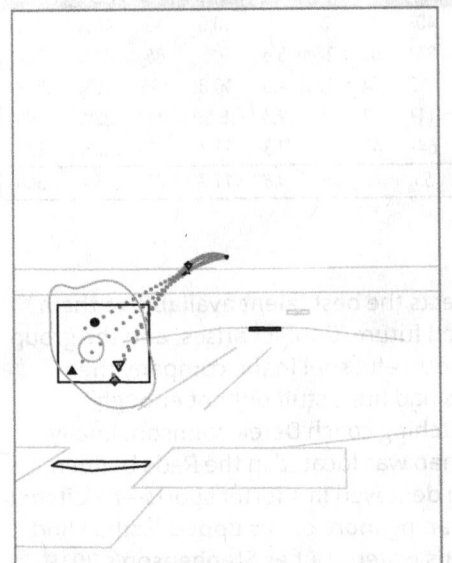

Pitch Shape vs RHH

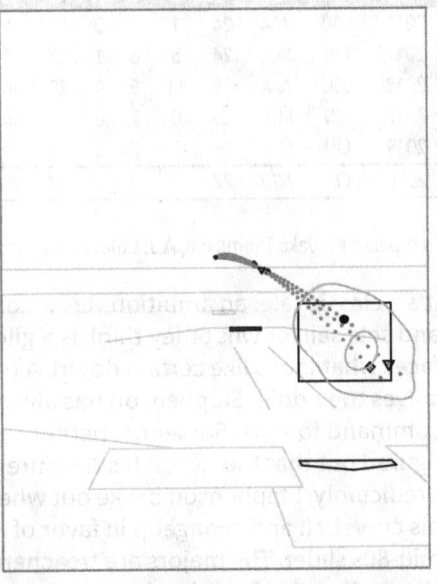

Type	Frequency	Velocity	H Movement	V Movement
● Fastball	50.5%	93.6 [103]	-7.6 [97]	-13 [108]
☐ Sinker				
+ Cutter				
▲ Changeup	5.6%	86.7 [105]	-12.7 [93]	-30.6 [91]
✕ Splitter				
▽ Slider	22.5%	83.1 [94]	10.3 [122]	-32.7 [101]
◇ Curveball	21.3%	81.6 [110]	11.2 [115]	-40.5 [115]
⊕ Slow Curveball				
✻ Knuckleball				
▼ Screwball				

Robert Stephenson RHP

Born: 02/24/93 Age: 27 Bats: R Throws: R
Height: 6'3" Weight: 215 Origin: Round 1, 2011 Draft (#27 overall)

YEAR	TEAM	LVL	AGE	W	L	SV	G	GS	IP	H	HR	BB/9	K/9	K	GB%	BABIP
2017	LOU	AAA	24	1	2	0	8	7	40¹	27	8	2.9	10.0	45	40%	.200
2017	CIN	MLB	24	5	6	1	25	11	84²	81	12	5.6	9.1	86	41%	.300
2018	LOU	AAA	25	11	6	0	20	20	113	74	12	4.5	10.8	135	38%	.239
2018	CIN	MLB	25	0	2	0	4	3	11²	17	2	9.3	8.5	11	32%	.395
2019	CIN	MLB	26	3	2	0	57	0	64²	43	9	3.3	11.3	81	33%	.231
2020	CIN	MLB	27	3	3	0	52	0	55	48	9	4.8	11.7	72	35%	.300

Comparables: Jake Thompson, A.J. Cole, Lucas Sims

It's a classic tale: an ambitious crew collects the best talent available to them and sets sail for what they think is a gilded future. Conflict arises, and the group faces what looks like certain doom. A resourceful soul in the company then solves the riddle. Stephenson has always had huge stuff but not enough command to start. Someone, perhaps pitching coach Derek Johnson, finally figured out that the "X" on his treasure map was located in the Reds bullpen. Predictably, Stephenson broke out when deployed in shorter spurts—he ditched his curveball and changeup in favor of leaning more on his upped fastball and mid-80s slider. The majors are treacherous waters, but as Stephenson's 2019 shows, there's often plunder to be had if you keep at it.

YEAR	TEAM	LVL	AGE	WHIP	ERA	DRA	WARP	MPH	FB%	WHF	CSP
2017	LOU	AAA	24	0.99	3.79	2.89	1.2				
2017	CIN	MLB	24	1.58	4.68	5.98	-0.5	96.6	54.2	13.5	43
2018	LOU	AAA	25	1.16	2.87	3.52	2.6				
2018	CIN	MLB	25	2.49	9.26	6.50	-0.2	95.2	36.4	11.3	47.2
2019	CIN	MLB	26	1.04	3.76	3.76	1.1	96.7	36.2	19.4	43.6
2020	CIN	MLB	27	1.40	4.33	4.31	0.7	96.1	44.3	16.3	45.2

Robert Stephenson, continued

Pitch Shape vs LHH   **Pitch Shape vs RHH**

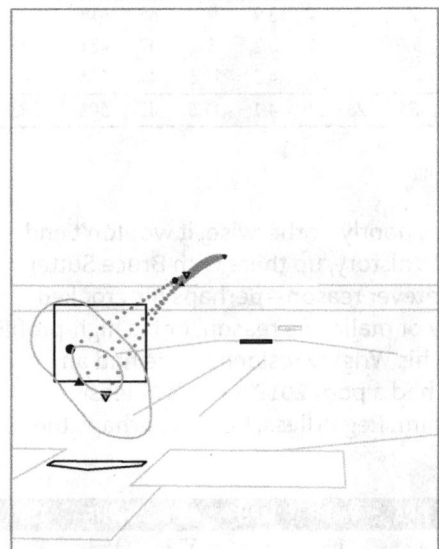 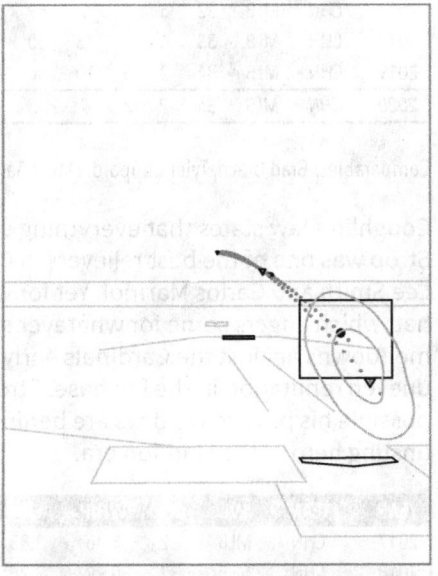

Type	Frequency	Velocity	H Movement	V Movement
● Fastball	36.2%	95.1 [108]	-9.1 [90]	-13.1 [107]
☐ Sinker				
+ Cutter				
▲ Changeup	6.7%	87.3 [107]	-6 [124]	-20.8 [119]
✕ Splitter				
▽ Slider	57.0%	84.7 [101]	4.3 [97]	-34.6 [96]
◇ Curveball				
✥ Slow Curveball				
✲ Knuckleball				
▼ Screwball				

Pedro Strop   RHP

Born: 06/13/85   Age: 35   Bats: R   Throws: R
Height: 6'1"   Weight: 220   Origin: International Free Agent, 2002

YEAR	TEAM	LVL	AGE	W	L	SV	G	GS	IP	H	HR	BB/9	K/9	K	GB%	BABIP
2017	CHN	MLB	32	5	4	0	69	0	60^1	45	4	3.9	9.7	65	61%	.270
2018	CHN	MLB	33	6	1	13	60	0	59^2	38	4	3.2	8.6	57	48%	.222
2019	CHN	MLB	34	2	5	10	50	0	41^2	33	6	4.3	10.6	49	54%	.276
2020	CHN	MLB	35	2	2	0	33	0	35	28	4	4.1	11.0	43	50%	.283

Comparables: Brad Brach, Tyler Clippard, David Aardsma

Coughlin's law states that everything ends poorly—otherwise, it wouldn't end. Strop was one of the best relievers in Cubs history, up there with Bruce Sutter, Lee Smith and Carlos Marmol. Yet for whatever reason—perhaps his crooked hat, which angers some for whatever silly or malicious reason, or his high-profile meltdowns against the Cardinals early in his Wrigley residency—he had an uneven reputation in the fan base. Strop had a poor 2019 and it's at least possible his productive days are behind him. Regardless, he was perhaps the unsung hero of the Maddon era.

YEAR	TEAM	LVL	AGE	WHIP	ERA	DRA	WARP	MPH	FB%	WHF	CSP
2017	CHN	MLB	32	1.18	2.83	3.23	1.3	97.6	55.7	16.3	43.1
2018	CHN	MLB	33	0.99	2.26	3.67	0.9	96.7	38.6	17	42.7
2019	CHN	MLB	34	1.27	4.97	3.66	0.8	95.3	36.7	14.5	40.5
2020	CHN	MLB	35	1.24	3.52	3.65	0.7	95.2	42.3	15.6	41.1

Pedro Strop, continued

Pitch Shape vs LHH

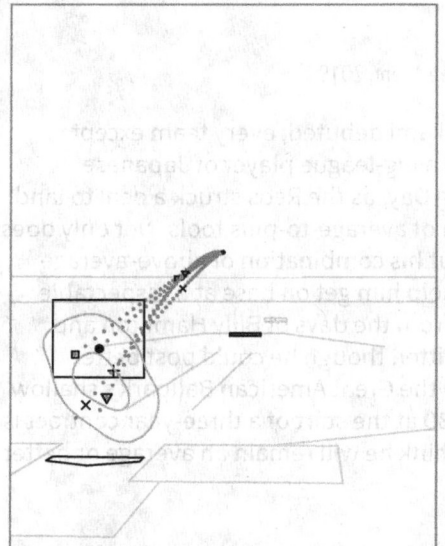

Pitch Shape vs RHH

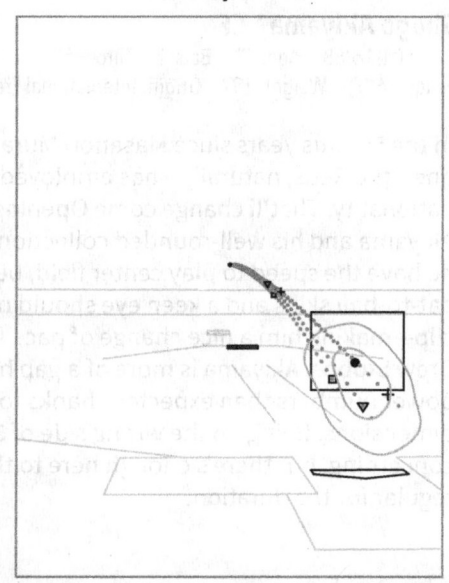

Type	Frequency	Velocity	H Movement	V Movement
● Fastball	23.3%	93.8 [104]	-3.5 [115]	-14.6 [103]
◻ Sinker	13.4%	93.8 [106]	-10.6 [113]	-17.5 [110]
+ Cutter	17.0%	88.6 [99]	3.5 [110]	-26 [93]
▲ Changeup				
✕ Splitter	5.3%	88.9 [116]	-9.4 [95]	-24.3 [116]
▽ Slider	41.0%	83.4 [96]	4.6 [98]	-37 [89]
◇ Curveball				
⊕ Slow Curveball				
✳ Knuckleball				
▼ Screwball				

Cincinnati Reds 2020

PLAYER COMMENTS WITHOUT GRAPHS

Shogo Akiyama   CF
Born: 04/16/88   Age: 32   Bats: L   Throws: R
Height: 6'0"   Weight: 187   Origin: International Free Agent, 2019

In the 50-plus years since Masanori Murakami debuted, every team except one—the Reds, naturally—has employed a big-league player of Japanese nationality. That'll change come Opening Day, as the Reds struck a deal to land Akiyama and his well-rounded collection of average-to-plus tools. Not only does he have the speed to play center field, but his combination of above-average bat-to-ball skills and a keen eye should help him get on base at a respectable clip—making him a nice change of pace from the days of Billy Hamilton and Drew Stubbs. Akiyama is more of a gap hitter, though he could post better power numbers than expected thanks to the Great American Ballpark's shallow dimensions. Being on the wrong side of 30 at the start of a three-year contract is concerning, but there's enough here to think he will remain an average or better regular for the duration.

Mariel Bautista   OF

Born: 10/15/97   Age: 22   Bats: R   Throws: R
Height: 6'3"   Weight: 194   Origin: International Free Agent, 2014

YEAR	TEAM	LVL	AGE	PA	R	2B	3B	HR	RBI	BB	K	SB	CS	AVG/OBP/SLG
2017	CIN	RK	19	157	29	9	1	0	20	5	24	16	1	.320/.353/.395
2018	BIL	RK	20	233	43	12	4	8	37	16	29	16	3	.330/.386/.541
2019	DYT	A	21	433	43	10	2	8	33	28	88	19	11	.233/.303/.332
2020	CIN	MLB	22	251	22	11	1	4	23	12	66	4	2	.227/.276/.340

Comparables: Victor Robles, Aristides Aquino, Michael Hermosillo

The phrase that always gets used to excuse so-so performances from athletic youngsters is "don't scout the stat line." Applying it to Bautista makes sense, given he shows the potential for five tools that grade as average or better—with the hit, power and speed comprising the "better" part. At some point projection has to materialize; otherwise, it's just phantom potential. Unfortunately, Bautista is nearing *that* point while remaining raw enough to threaten salmonella poisoning. He's too old for rookie ball, but not mature enough as a player to succeed in A-ball, let alone higher up. Something's going to have to give—either he's going to make The Jump, or he's going to fall into the non-prospect void. Check back in a year for the conclusion.

YEAR	TEAM	LVL	AGE	PA	DRC+	VORP	BABIP	BRR	FRAA	WARP
2017	CIN	RK	19	157	119	14.8	.379	3.5	LF(24): -1.7, CF(10): 3.2	1.1
2018	BIL	RK	20	233	139	28.0	.349	2.3	CF(40): -4.4, LF(6): -1.3	0.6
2019	DYT	A	21	433	88	5.5	.278	1.9	LF(42): -3.0, RF(36): 0.9	0.2
2020	CIN	MLB	22	251	64	-3.6	.298	0.1	LF -1, CF -1	-0.5

Christian Colón INF

Born: 05/14/89   Age: 31   Bats: R   Throws: R
Height: 5'10"   Weight: 195   Origin: Round 1, 2010 Draft (#4 overall)

YEAR	TEAM	LVL	AGE	PA	R	2B	3B	HR	RBI	BB	K	SB	CS	AVG/OBP/SLG
2017	NWO	AAA	28	177	17	8	0	1	13	16	26	6	3	.302/.379/.376
2017	KCA	MLB	28	19	1	0	0	0	0	1	3	0	0	.176/.222/.176
2017	MIA	MLB	28	38	3	1	0	0	0	4	7	0	0	.152/.243/.182
2018	GWN	AAA	29	55	3	0	0	0	3	4	8	1	0	.204/.278/.204
2018	LVG	AAA	29	313	44	22	1	6	38	36	30	11	5	.304/.396/.459
2019	LOU	AAA	30	582	63	37	2	10	70	57	58	24	13	.300/.372/.443
2019	CIN	MLB	30	8	1	0	0	0	1	0	0	0	0	.500/.625/.500
2020	CIN	MLB	31	251	23	9	0	4	23	20	38	5	2	.230/.300/.328

Comparables: Adam Kennedy, Marlon Anderson, Mickey Morandini

Colón joined his fifth organization in 2019, making him fit for the "journeyman" title. Along the way, he's piled up thousands of professional plate appearances that suggest he's a slap-hitting, up-and-down infielder who is useful only in an emergency. The Reds have had some successes coaxing power out of unexpected places—Eugenio Suárez, Scooter Gennett and Zack Cozart come to mind—so you never want to say never. Even so, we're comfortable in our assessment that he's just a depth piece, his draft pedigree serving as little more than a trivial footnote.

YEAR	TEAM	LVL	AGE	PA	DRC+	VORP	BABIP	BRR	FRAA	WARP
2017	NWO	AAA	28	177	106	9.9	.358	-1.5	3B(17): -2.0, 2B(16): 0.4	0.3
2017	KCA	MLB	28	19	66	-2.1	.214	0.1	2B(6): 0.8	0.1
2017	MIA	MLB	28	38	64	-2.1	.192	0.4	3B(10): 0.7, 2B(4): 0.3	0.1
2018	GWN	AAA	29	55	56	-3.4	.244	-0.5	2B(14): 1.1	0.0
2018	LVG	AAA	29	313	122	14.9	.323	-0.9	2B(43): 4.5, 3B(25): 0.9	2.2
2019	LOU	AAA	30	582	110	28.6	.315	-2.4	3B(104): 12.6, SS(15): -1.7	3.4
2019	CIN	MLB	30	8	92	0.2	.500	-0.4	2B(3): 0.0	0.0
2020	CIN	MLB	31	251	70	-2.0	.260	-0.3	3B 1, 2B 1	0.0

Phillip Ervin OF

Born: 07/15/92 Age: 27 Bats: R Throws: R
Height: 5'10" Weight: 207 Origin: Round 1, 2013 Draft (#27 overall)

YEAR	TEAM	LVL	AGE	PA	R	2B	3B	HR	RBI	BB	K	SB	CS	AVG/OBP/SLG
2017	LOU	AAA	24	408	46	20	2	7	40	37	83	23	6	.256/.328/.380
2017	CIN	MLB	24	64	8	2	0	3	10	4	15	4	1	.259/.317/.448
2018	LOU	AAA	25	202	25	12	4	5	38	20	39	10	7	.289/.373/.491
2018	CIN	MLB	25	247	27	10	1	7	31	20	60	6	1	.252/.324/.404
2019	LOU	AAA	26	172	27	8	1	6	26	19	34	6	6	.290/.384/.483
2019	CIN	MLB	26	260	30	11	7	7	23	18	63	4	3	.271/.331/.466
2020	CIN	MLB	27	91	11	4	1	3	11	8	22	4	1	.240/.319/.422

Comparables: Tyler Collins, Mo Vaughn, Desmond Jennings

Ervin has been on prospect radars since he was drafted 27th in 2013—or, a handful of spots ahead of a different right-handed collegiate outfielder named Aaron Judge. Whoops. While Judge has since solidified himself as one of the best hitters in the game, Ervin is still trying to establish a foothold on a roster spot. His time is coming. He's hit .313/.371/.536 in his first 200 plate appearances against lefties, and no longer has minor-league options remaining. Presuming teams don't do something ridiculous with the 26-player roster—like, say, carry 14 pitchers at a time—Ervin should spend at least a few seasons on bench.

YEAR	TEAM	LVL	AGE	PA	DRC+	VORP	BABIP	BRR	FRAA	WARP
2017	LOU	AAA	24	408	99	7.7	.315	0.6	LF(56): 8.7, CF(40): -3.1	1.6
2017	CIN	MLB	24	64	96	4.7	.300	1.1	CF(9): -0.6, RF(5): -0.4	0.2
2018	LOU	AAA	25	202	136	14.7	.341	-0.8	LF(37): 5.2, CF(8): -0.5	1.6
2018	CIN	MLB	25	247	96	6.4	.310	1.0	LF(39): 0.2, RF(33): -2.7	0.3
2019	LOU	AAA	26	172	135	14.7	.333	2.0	CF(25): 0.9, LF(10): 1.2	1.5
2019	CIN	MLB	26	260	94	6.1	.339	1.0	LF(61): -5.5, CF(25): 1.1	0.2
2020	CIN	MLB	27	91	96	2.8	.289	0.2	CF 0, RF 0	0.3

TJ Friedl OF

Born: 08/14/95 Age: 24 Bats: L Throws: L
Height: 5'10" Weight: 180 Origin: Undrafted Free Agent, 2016

YEAR	TEAM	LVL	AGE	PA	R	2B	3B	HR	RBI	BB	K	SB	CS	AVG/OBP/SLG
2017	DYT	A	21	292	47	20	6	5	25	29	46	14	8	.284/.378/.472
2017	DAY	A+	21	199	15	6	2	2	13	10	39	2	1	.257/.313/.346
2018	DAY	A+	22	274	40	10	4	3	35	38	44	11	4	.294/.405/.412
2018	PEN	AA	22	296	47	10	3	2	16	28	56	19	5	.276/.359/.360
2019	CHT	AA	23	269	38	11	4	5	28	29	50	13	4	.235/.347/.385
2020	CIN	MLB	24	251	24	11	2	5	25	20	60	6	2	.227/.305/.363

Comparables: Matt Szczur, Ty France, Zoilo Almonte

Friedl, who signed in 2016 as an undrafted free agent out of University of Nevada-Reno, has since outplayed plenty of players who were more highly thought of as amateurs. You can probably guess what kind of skill set he has based on that alone. If you said some combination of "fourth outfielder," "high-motor," "good eye," "good speed" and/or "no power," then congratulations—you win. He didn't hit as well as one might hope in a second look at Double-A. But, as we like to say around here, once you've made it to Double-A you're only a phone call away from the majors. For a player with Friedl's background, making it this far is already a win.

YEAR	TEAM	LVL	AGE	PA	DRC+	VORP	BABIP	BRR	FRAA	WARP
2017	DYT	A	21	292	138	25.6	.328	4.1	RF(22): 0.7, CF(18): -3.0	1.9
2017	DAY	A+	21	199	80	3.3	.317	0.0	CF(20): -1.3, RF(18): -2.5	0.2
2018	DAY	A+	22	274	138	23.4	.350	4.7	LF(39): 2.0, CF(19): -1.0	2.3
2018	PEN	AA	22	296	112	12.7	.345	3.3	LF(53): 5.1, CF(9): -1.0	1.9
2019	CHT	AA	23	269	113	9.4	.277	1.3	RF(42): 2.4, LF(14): -1.4	1.1
2020	CIN	MLB	24	251	79	1.6	.286	0.4	LF 2, CF -2	0.2

Jonathan India 3B
Born: 12/15/96 Age: 23 Bats: R Throws: R
Height: 6'0" Weight: 200 Origin: Round 1, 2018 Draft (#5 overall)

YEAR	TEAM	LVL	AGE	PA	R	2B	3B	HR	RBI	BB	K	SB	CS	AVG/OBP/SLG
2018	GRV	RK	21	62	11	2	1	3	12	15	12	1	0	.261/.452/.543
2018	DYT	A	21	112	17	7	0	3	11	13	28	5	0	.229/.339/.396
2019	DAY	A+	22	367	50	15	5	8	30	37	84	7	5	.256/.346/.410
2019	CHT	AA	22	145	24	3	0	3	14	22	26	4	0	.270/.414/.378
2020	CIN	MLB	23	251	28	11	1	8	29	25	70	4	1	.231/.326/.399

Comparables: Alex Blandino, Hunter Dozier, Kyle Kubitza

The Reds were evidently so happy with Nick Senzel that they took the Coke Zero version, in India, two drafts later at No. 5. Like Senzel, India has a slick glove at third with enough athleticism to cover short or second in a pinch; he also has a contact-over-power offensive profile, and so on and so forth. We could keep going, but you get the point: it's similar, just less of. Teams have done worse with higher draft picks than what India projects to become, which is a totally fine third baseman who could reach the majors in 2020.

YEAR	TEAM	LVL	AGE	PA	DRC+	VORP	BABIP	BRR	FRAA	WARP
2018	GRV	RK	21	62	150	6.3	.290	0.6	3B(12): -0.6, SS(2): -0.2	0.5
2018	DYT	A	21	112	104	7.0	.292	1.5	3B(21): 2.4, SS(4): -0.1	0.8
2019	DAY	A+	22	367	130	18.1	.319	-1.8	3B(74): -9.2, 2B(5): 0.0	1.0
2019	CHT	AA	22	145	141	11.0	.314	0.2	3B(31): -0.4	1.1
2020	CIN	MLB	23	251	95	6.5	.303	-0.1	3B -2, SS 0	0.4

Travis Jankowski OF

Born: 06/15/91 Age: 29 Bats: L Throws: R
Height: 6'2" Weight: 185 Origin: Round 1, 2012 Draft (#44 overall)

YEAR	TEAM	LVL	AGE	PA	R	2B	3B	HR	RBI	BB	K	SB	CS	AVG/OBP/SLG
2017	ELP	AAA	26	157	20	5	1	0	11	18	28	8	1	.266/.350/.317
2017	SDN	MLB	26	87	10	2	0	0	1	9	28	4	0	.187/.282/.213
2018	ELP	AAA	27	94	17	4	0	1	11	11	21	4	3	.363/.452/.450
2018	SDN	MLB	27	387	45	12	3	4	17	37	73	24	7	.259/.332/.346
2019	ELP	AAA	28	183	27	6	0	0	12	21	32	7	2	.313/.393/.350
2019	SDN	MLB	28	24	4	0	0	0	0	2	4	2	2	.182/.250/.182
2020	CIN	MLB	29	77	7	2	0	1	6	7	18	4	1	.241/.317/.314

Comparables: Dexter Fowler, Herm Winningham, A.J. Pollock

There isn't much to say about Jankowski's lost 2019 season, as the fleet outfielder with the flowing blond locks missed much of it with a fractured wrist suffered when attempting a diving catch in March, then ping-ponged between San Diego and El Paso while the Friars sorted through their outfield logjam. You already know his game (serious speed, reasonable center field defense, high energy, no power) and his optimal role (fifth outfielder and pinch runner). But did you know his nickname is "Freddy" due to his daily childhood dose of *Mister Rogers' Neighborhood*? Makes you wonder whether every time Jankowski swipes a bag or runs down a gapper he hears a voice in his head repeating "Speedy Delivery!" Jankowski will compete for a big-league bench role with Cincinnati this spring.

YEAR	TEAM	LVL	AGE	PA	DRC+	VORP	BABIP	BRR	FRAA	WARP
2017	ELP	AAA	26	157	75	1.4	.333	0.1	CF(22): -1.7, LF(7): -0.3	-0.2
2017	SDN	MLB	26	87	53	-3.1	.298	0.9	LF(19): -0.4, CF(4): 0.3	-0.2
2018	ELP	AAA	27	94	112	8.8	.483	1.5	CF(20): 2.5	0.9
2018	SDN	MLB	27	387	79	8.6	.319	4.5	RF(58): 3.3, CF(34): -1.7	0.4
2019	ELP	AAA	28	183	92	2.4	.388	0.8	CF(18): -2.2, RF(10): -0.5	0.2
2019	SDN	MLB	28	24	78	0.2	.222	0.7	CF(5): 0.5, RF(5): -0.1	0.1
2020	CIN	MLB	29	77	72	-0.6	.319	0.5	RF 2	0.2

Braylin Minier SS
Born: 06/11/03   Age: 17   Bats: L   Throws: R
Height: 6'0"   Weight: 160   Origin: International Free Agent, 2019

A Dominican-born shortstop, Minier turned 16 about three weeks before signing with the Reds for a $1.8 million bonus on July 2. Seeing as how he's years away from playing stateside, we could write just about anything here and have it fly. We'll pass on abusing your trust in us to offer the truth: we have no idea at this point if Minier will stick at shortstop, grow into his frame enough to hit for power, or hit on 16 during a friendly clubhouse game of blackjack. In four years, we'll know a little more.

Cincinnati Reds 2020

Michael Siani CF
Born: 07/16/99 Age: 20 Bats: L Throws: L
Height: 6'1" Weight: 188 Origin: Round 4, 2018 Draft (#109 overall)

YEAR	TEAM	LVL	AGE	PA	R	2B	3B	HR	RBI	BB	K	SB	CS	AVG/OBP/SLG
2018	GRV	RK	18	205	24	6	3	2	13	16	35	6	4	.288/.351/.386
2019	DYT	A	19	531	75	10	6	6	39	46	109	45	15	.253/.333/.339
2020	CIN	MLB	20	251	22	10	1	4	22	16	65	4	2	.231/.289/.329

Comparables: Kyle Tucker, Abraham Almonte, Xavier Avery

The good: Siani won't turn 21 until July and hit .350/.412/.483 over his final 15 games of the season. The bad: he had a disappointing season overall and looks like a fourth outfielder at best. The worst: his brother, Sammy, was drafted 70-something picks earlier this year—ruining Thanksgiving by ensuring that he doesn't even have family bragging rights to fall back on.

YEAR	TEAM	LVL	AGE	PA	DRC+	VORP	BABIP	BRR	FRAA	WARP
2018	GRV	RK	18	205	115	10.8	.342	-0.1	CF(45): 6.5	1.6
2019	DYT	A	19	531	96	22.0	.318	7.4	CF(111): 24.7, RF(5): -0.7	4.8
2020	CIN	MLB	20	251	66	-2.5	.306	0.4	CF 6, RF 0	0.3

Tyler Stephenson   C

Born: 08/16/96   Age: 23   Bats: R   Throws: R
Height: 6'4"   Weight: 225   Origin: Round 1, 2015 Draft (#11 overall)

YEAR	TEAM	LVL	AGE	PA	R	2B	3B	HR	RBI	BB	K	SB	CS	AVG/OBP/SLG
2017	DYT	A	20	348	39	22	0	6	50	44	58	2	1	.278/.374/.414
2018	DAY	A+	21	450	60	20	1	11	59	45	98	1	0	.250/.338/.392
2019	CHT	AA	22	363	47	19	1	6	44	37	60	0	0	.285/.372/.410
2020	CIN	MLB	23	251	26	13	0	7	29	19	63	0	0	.240/.309/.396

Comparables: Christian Vázquez, Victor Caratini, Meibrys Viloria

The Reds have had a lot of high first-round picks in recent years, and they've used them on a variety of different player types. There's Senzel and India (safe collegiate hitters), Lodolo (a stud lefty from a major conference) and Greene (an explosive prep arm). There's also Stephenson, who hails from perhaps the riskiest pool of them all as a prep catcher. Extremely tall and injury prone, Stephenson still grades well as a defender. He also, as an added bonus, just posted a strong effort showing in Double-A last season. There's obvious attrition potential here—he might get hurt some more, or he might prove unable to hit big-league pitching—but there's also a real chance he's going to be at least a reserve backstop. All things considered, that's a win.

YEAR	TEAM	P. COUNT	FRM RUNS	BLK RUNS	THRW RUNS	TOT RUNS
2019	CHT	11672	-11.5	0.0	-1.2	-12.5
2020	CIN	9182	-6.8	-0.5	-0.5	-7.8

YEAR	TEAM	LVL	AGE	PA	DRC+	VORP	BABIP	BRR	FRAA	WARP
2017	DYT	A	20	348	138	20.4	.322	-2.6	C(53): -4.0	2.0
2018	DAY	A+	21	450	118	24.3	.301	0.2	C(97): -3.3	2.4
2019	CHT	AA	22	363	128	23.3	.331	-2.1	C(85): -11.8	1.3
2020	CIN	MLB	23	251	86	3.0	.300	-0.5	C -8	-0.5

Cincinnati Reds 2020

Michel Triana   INF
Born: 11/23/99   Age: 20   Bats: L   Throws: R
Height: 6'3"   Weight: 230   Origin: International Free Agent, 2019

One thinks of July 2nd signings as all belonging to the same archetype: incredibly raw, athletic 16-year-olds. Triana received a $1.3 million bonus, but the above description doesn't apply to him. Rather, this season will represent his age-20 campaign, and he's likely to end up at first base over the long haul—suggesting he's going to have to hit to make up for his lacking physicality and reach the majors. The odds are, of course, very much against him. In that sense, Triana *is* a typical July 2nd signing.

José De León RHP

Born: 08/07/92 Age: 27 Bats: R Throws: R
Height: 6'1" Weight: 220 Origin: Round 24, 2013 Draft (#724 overall)

YEAR	TEAM	LVL	AGE	W	L	SV	G	GS	IP	H	HR	BB/9	K/9	K	GB%	BABIP
2017	RAY	RK	24	1	0	0	3	2	12	4	1	0.8	9.0	12	30%	.115
2017	PCH	A+	24	1	0	0	4	3	14¹	11	0	5.7	11.3	18	39%	.333
2017	DUR	AAA	24	0	2	0	3	3	12	14	1	4.5	10.5	14	38%	.394
2017	TBA	MLB	24	1	0	0	1	0	2²	4	1	10.1	6.8	2	60%	.333
2019	DUR	AAA	26	2	1	1	17	13	51¹	41	4	4.7	12.8	73	30%	.330
2019	TBA	MLB	26	1	0	0	3	0	4	3	0	6.8	15.8	7	44%	.333
2020	CIN	MLB	27	2	2	0	42	0	44	37	7	3.9	8.5	42	35%	.259

Comparables: Rafael Montero, Ryan Helsley, Dan Straily

Turn ahead a few chapters and read most of what was written about Anthony Banda. Go ahead, take a minute. Oh, hey! Welcome back. Much of the same can be said for De León, who also returned from Tommy John surgery with minimal impact to the Rays. He still has a low-90s fastball that he backs with a very good off-speed pitch in his change. De León also figures to be in that hybrid mix of probably not good enough for 200 innings, but more talented than 50 standard reliever frames. He is certainly worth the flier the Reds took on him this winter.

YEAR	TEAM	LVL	AGE	WHIP	ERA	DRA	WARP	MPH	FB%	WHF	CSP
2017	RAY	RK	24	0.42	0.75	0.66	0.7				
2017	PCH	A+	24	1.40	1.88	3.93	0.2				
2017	DUR	AAA	24	1.67	6.75	5.31	0.1				
2017	TBA	MLB	24	2.62	10.12	6.15	0.0	93.3	60.3	8.8	47.1
2019	DUR	AAA	26	1.32	3.51	3.80	1.4				
2019	TBA	MLB	26	1.50	2.25	3.10	0.1	94.8	57.5	21.3	49
2020	CIN	MLB	27	1.27	3.95	4.05	0.7	93.9	59.1	17.3	48.9

Hunter Greene   RHP

Born: 08/06/99   Age: 20   Bats: R   Throws: R
Height: 6'4"   Weight: 215   Origin: Round 1, 2017 Draft (#2 overall)

YEAR	TEAM	LVL	AGE	W	L	SV	G	GS	IP	H	HR	BB/9	K/9	K	GB%	BABIP
2018	DYT	A	18	3	7	0	18	18	68¹	66	6	3.0	11.7	89	43%	.353
2020	CIN	MLB	20	2	2	0	33	0	35	36	6	4.2	9.1	35	40%	.310

Comparables: Jordan Lyles, Roberto Osuna, Mike Soroka

Greene arrived in professional baseball as one of the most hyped prep prospects in recent memory. A dazzling two-way talent with a big-time arm who probably would've been picked in the first round as a shortstop had he played only that side of the ball. Yet in the time since he was drafted, he's encountered all the snags that tend to derail young pitching prospects—beginning with struggles based on his limited, fastball-heavy arsenal, and extending to health woes that culminated in Tommy John surgery. Greene should be back on the mound come 2020 and here's hoping that his arm strength, athleticism and aptitude will get his stock moving in the right direction. We're certainly not ready to move on from or dismiss him as a bust.

YEAR	TEAM	LVL	AGE	WHIP	ERA	DRA	WARP	MPH	FB%	WHF	CSP
2018	DYT	A	18	1.30	4.48	4.58	0.5				
2020	CIN	MLB	20	1.49	5.13	5.13	0.1				

Vladimir Gutierrez   RHP

Born: 09/18/95   Age: 24   Bats: R   Throws: R
Height: 6'0"   Weight: 190   Origin: International Free Agent, 2016

YEAR	TEAM	LVL	AGE	W	L	SV	G	GS	IP	H	HR	BB/9	K/9	K	GB%	BABIP
2017	DAY	A+	21	7	8	0	19	19	103	108	10	1.7	8.2	94	42%	.320
2018	PEN	AA	22	9	10	0	27	27	147	139	18	2.3	8.9	145	46%	.298
2019	LOU	AAA	23	6	11	0	27	27	137	144	26	3.2	7.7	117	41%	.291
2020	CIN	MLB	24	2	2	0	33	0	35	37	7	3.6	6.9	27	41%	.287

Comparables: José Ureña, Hunter Wood, Jackson Stephens

Gutierrez stands at 6-foot even and has a gigantic spider tattooed on his throat. Those two tidbits should be all you need to know in order to guess he's probably headed for the bullpen. (Hey, you have to be wired a little differently to succeed in relief.) Sure enough, that outcome seems more likely following his struggles in Triple-A with the rabbit ball (his home run rate spiked and his ERA went with it). The fastball sits in the 92-94 mph range and his main putaway pitch is a curveball that he can manipulate to different effects. He's likely to be a fine middle-relief type, just nothing special. In a sense, then, Gutierrez almost feels like something of a throwback. He would have been a dominant sensation if he had arrived in the '90s, but will probably be just another pitcher these days—albeit just another pitcher who has an enormous spider guarding his windpipe.

YEAR	TEAM	LVL	AGE	WHIP	ERA	DRA	WARP	MPH	FB%	WHF	CSP
2017	DAY	A+	21	1.23	4.46	3.84	1.7				
2018	PEN	AA	22	1.20	4.35	4.18	2.0				
2019	LOU	AAA	23	1.40	6.04	4.93	2.4				
2020	CIN	MLB	24	1.45	5.32	5.34	0.0				

Nick Lodolo LHP

Born: 02/05/98 Age: 22 Bats: L Throws: L
Height: 6'6" Weight: 202 Origin: Round 1, 2019 Draft (#7 overall)

YEAR	TEAM	LVL	AGE	W	L	SV	G	GS	IP	H	HR	BB/9	K/9	K	GB%	BABIP
2019	BIL	RK+	21	0	1	0	6	6	11^1	12	1	0.0	16.7	21	36%	.458
2019	DYT	A	21	0	0	0	2	2	7	6	0	0.0	11.6	9	50%	.333
2020	CIN	MLB	22	2	2	0	33	0	35	35	5	3.6	8.2	32	43%	.295

Comparables: Josh Rogers, Devin Smeltzer, Eric Surkamp

The first pitcher selected in June's draft, Lodolo hails from TCU and possesses an alluring frame (he's tall and lanky) and arsenal (led mid-90s heat and a potential breaking ball). As is often the case with very good, not elite pitching prospects, he needs to continue to refine his command and his changeup. All pitchers carry a certain amount of risk, and Lord knows the Reds have whiffed more than they've hit on pitchers, but Lodolo looks like he could be a quality one—and a fast-moving one, at that.

YEAR	TEAM	LVL	AGE	WHIP	ERA	DRA	WARP	MPH	FB%	WHF	CSP
2019	BIL	RK+	21	1.06	2.38	2.41	0.5				
2019	DYT	A	21	0.86	2.57	3.40	0.1				
2020	CIN	MLB	22	1.39	4.64	4.82	0.2				

Cody Reed   LHP

Born: 04/15/93   Age: 27   Bats: L   Throws: L
Height: 6'5"   Weight: 230   Origin: Round 2, 2013 Draft (#46 overall)

YEAR	TEAM	LVL	AGE	W	L	SV	G	GS	IP	H	HR	BB/9	K/9	K	GB%	BABIP
2017	LOU	AAA	24	4	9	0	21	20	106^1	105	7	5.2	8.6	102	50%	.328
2017	CIN	MLB	24	1	1	1	12	1	17^2	11	3	9.7	8.7	17	65%	.200
2018	LOU	AAA	25	4	8	0	18	17	105^2	109	13	2.6	8.9	105	46%	.325
2018	CIN	MLB	25	1	3	0	17	7	43	45	5	3.1	8.8	42	63%	.323
2019	LOU	AAA	26	1	2	0	18	0	20^2	13	1	3.5	10.9	25	70%	.267
2019	CIN	MLB	26	0	0	0	3	0	6^1	6	0	1.4	9.9	7	76%	.353
2020	CIN	MLB	27	2	2	0	42	0	44	48	7	3.4	7.9	39	61%	.312

Comparables: Brian Flynn, John Gant, Aaron Blair

The Reds finally gave up the ghost on Reed as a starter. Fortunately, he seemed to take well to life in short spurts by better leveraging his best pitches and…yes, this reads like a half-dozen other comments in this chapter. What can we say? Cincinnati hasn't done much to develop quality starters, but if 2019 is any indication they should have a small fleet of cheap relievers. There's some value in that.

YEAR	TEAM	LVL	AGE	WHIP	ERA	DRA	WARP	MPH	FB%	WHF	CSP
2017	LOU	AAA	24	1.56	3.55	5.43	0.3				
2017	CIN	MLB	24	1.70	5.09	4.82	0.1	96.8	51.2	13.9	40.4
2018	LOU	AAA	25	1.32	3.92	5.42	0.1				
2018	CIN	MLB	25	1.40	3.98	4.36	0.4	95.4	50.2	11	48.1
2019	LOU	AAA	26	1.02	2.61	2.81	0.7				
2019	CIN	MLB	26	1.11	1.42	3.17	0.2	96.6	55.2	15.5	55.6
2020	CIN	MLB	27	1.45	4.97	4.92	0.2	95.4	51.4	12.2	49.9

Cincinnati Reds 2020

LINEOUTS

Hitters

HITTER	POS	TEAM	LVL	AGE	PA	R	2B	3B	HR	RBI	BB	K	SB	CS	AVG/OBP/SLG	DRC+	WARP
Tyler Callihan	2B	GRV	Rk+	19	217	27	10	5	5	26	9	46	9	3	.250/.286/.422	86	0.3
Stuart Fairchild	CF	DAY	A+	23	281	32	17	2	8	37	25	60	3	5	.258/.335/.440	148	1.9
	CF	CHT	AA	23	179	25	12	1	4	17	19	23	3	2	.275/.380/.444	132	1.2
Kyle Farmer	UT	CIN	MLB	28	197	22	6	0	9	27	10	59	4	1	.230/.279/.410	76	-0.2
Jose Garcia	SS	DAY	A+	21	452	58	37	1	8	55	25	83	15	2	.280/.343/.436	143	3.8
Juan Graterol	C	CIN	MLB	30	18	1	0	0	0	1	0	4	0	0	.222/.222/.222	75	0.0
	C	LOU	AAA	30	226	19	8	1	2	26	14	18	0	1	.249/.301/.325	68	-0.9
Jameson Hannah	CF	STO	A+	21	414	48	25	3	2	31	29	88	6	7	.283/.341/.381	111	0.7
	CF	DAY	A+	21	78	6	3	1	0	6	9	16	2	1	.224/.325/.299	70	-0.1
Alfredo Rodriguez	MI	CHT	AA	25	436	50	18	2	1	25	22	62	13	9	.286/.325/.347	93	1.6
	MI	LOU	AAA	25	88	5	4	0	0	9	7	13	3	0	.169/.261/.221	56	0.1
Andy Sugilio	OF	DAY	A+	22	485	57	11	5	3	39	24	92	23	11	.294/.331/.360	115	1.5

A name for the deepest of dynasty players, July 2nd signing **Deivid Alcantara** is a teenage outfielder who can really run. We may see him in the majors in 2025 or so. We probably won't. ⓧ Drafted in the third round but paid a second-round signing bonus, **Tyler Callihan** is a big and (somewhat older) prep infielder who is already flashing serious power and swing-and-miss potential in rookie ball. ⓧ Typically, guys who float through the minors doing a little bit of everything offensively without any standout carrying tool are playing with fire. **Stuart Fairchild** distinguishes himself from that group with his ability to play a good center field. ⓧ A product of these bullpen-laden times, C/1B/2B/3B **Kyle Farmer** is about as exciting and necessary as a quarter-rest in a musical score. You may look at his production and come away underwhelmed, but then, you may also have tried playing rec-league softball with a team of eight players. ⓧ For a minute it looked like **Jose Garcia**, a $5 million Cuban signing, was going to be only a slick-fielding shortstop and nothing more. He broke out in 2019, hitting for surprisingly decent power in a tough environment in High-A. ⓧ **Juan Graterol** has appeared in 10 major-league games across the last two seasons and serves as an answer to the question, "What is a replacement-level catcher?" The Twins will find out for themselves. ⓧ Find yourself someone who loves you as much as the Reds love hit-over-power fourth outfielders who can handle center. On a related note, Cincy made sure to grab **Jameson Hannah** from the Athletics as the return on Tanner Roark. ⓧ Technically drafted as a shortstop, **Rece Hinds** played in three professional games after signing - each as a third baseman. His calling card is a whole lot of power, but it's anyone's guess as to how much he'll tap into. ⓧ The Reds like to find good defensive infielders and teach them how to access some power. Pulling that trick with **Alfredo Rodriguez** has thus far proved to be beyond their reach. ⓧ The FSL is a tough place to hit, meaning **Andy Sugilio**'s 2019 was better than it looks. He'll try again to break out in 2020, just like the Baha Men will keep searching for another hit record.

Pitchers

PITCHER	TEAM	LVL	AGE	W	L	SV	G	GS	IP	H	HR	BB/9	K/9	K	GB%	WHIP	ERA	DRA	WARP
R.J. Alaniz	TAC	AAA	28	2	1	2	10	0	12^2	18	3	5.0	16.3	23	42%	1.97	6.39	4.08	0.3
	LOU	AAA	28	1	2	4	25	0	27^2	25	1	3.6	10.1	31	50%	1.30	2.93	3.18	0.8
	SEA	MLB	28	0	0	0	4	0	4	11	3	6.8	13.5	6	44%	3.50	20.25	5.84	0.0
	CIN	MLB	28	1	0	0	8	0	11^2	8	0	3.1	5.4	7	46%	1.03	5.40	5.55	0.0
Tejay Antone	CHT	AA	25	7	4	0	13	13	74^2	63	4	2.7	7.6	63	60%	1.14	3.38	4.21	0.7
	LOU	AAA	25	4	8	0	14	13	71^2	93	7	3.9	8.8	70	52%	1.73	4.65	6.51	0.1
Matt Bowman	LOU	AAA	28	1	1	4	29	0	39	28	1	4.2	8.1	35	55%	1.18	2.08	3.78	0.9
	CIN	MLB	28	2	0	0	27	0	32	27	2	3.7	7.0	25	56%	1.25	3.66	4.92	0.2
Ryan Hendrix	CHT	AA	24	3	0	2	16	0	19^1	14	0	3.7	10.7	23	46%	1.14	2.33	4.00	0.1
Keury Mella	LOU	AAA	25	8	14	0	27	27	142^2	160	22	3.5	6.4	102	53%	1.51	5.05	5.38	1.8
	CIN	MLB	25	0	0	0	2	0	3^2	5	0	4.9	9.8	4	33%	1.91	7.36	4.87	0.0
Packy Naughton	DAY	A+	23	5	2	0	9	9	51^1	49	2	1.6	8.8	50	45%	1.13	2.63	4.20	0.5
	CHT	AA	23	6	10	0	19	19	105^2	109	8	2.2	6.9	81	40%	1.28	3.66	4.91	0.1
Lyon Richardson	DYT	A	19	3	9	0	26	26	112^2	126	10	2.6	8.5	106	41%	1.41	4.15	5.70	-0.7
Tony Santillan	CHT	AA	22	2	8	0	21	21	102^1	110	8	4.7	8.1	92	37%	1.60	4.84	5.75	-1.0
Josh Smith	COH	AAA	29	8	1	6	41	0	52^2	32	7	4.1	12.6	74	39%	1.06	2.73	2.43	1.9
	CLE	MLB	29	0	0	0	8	0	8^1	8	0	8.6	13.0	12	38%	1.92	5.40	5.06	0.0
	MIA	MLB	29	0	0	0	6	0	4^1	3	0	6.2	4.2	2	27%	1.38	8.31	7.83	-0.1
Jackson Stephens	LOU	AAA	25	8	4	0	47	2	84	93	6	4.0	8.6	80	52%	1.55	5.14	4.46	1.5
Tyler Thornburg	PAW	AAA	30	0	2	0	11	1	10^2	17	5	7.6	11.0	13	29%	2.44	12.66	8.52	-0.2
	OKL	AAA	30	0	0	0	12	0	12	11	3	6.8	11.2	15	26%	1.67	6.00	3.95	0.3
	BOS	MLB	30	0	0	0	16	0	18^2	21	4	4.8	10.6	22	30%	1.66	7.71	6.51	-0.1

It's really, really cool that **R.J. Alaniz** - an undrafted free-agent in 2010 - made his major-league debut in 2019 at age 28. He got knocked around pretty hard and doesn't have surplus heat so it's going to take all he has to stick around. ⓧ The only thing that righty reliever prospect **Tejay Antone** loves more than spelling names phonetically is inducing ground balls—something he did more than half the time between Double- and Triple-A. ⓧ No. You're thinking of Michael Baumann, the prospect. No, not that one either, that's Michael Bowden, the old Red Sox prospect. Matt Barnes? Nah, he misses way more bats. This is **Matt Bowman**. He's pretty good. ⓧ **Ryan Hendrix** didn't pitch much in 2019, but he missed bats and allowed zero homers in Double-A. That's a recipe to get into the Reds house over yonder. ⚾ The Reds used **Keury Mella** as a starter throughout the minors, but he looks to have hit his head in Triple-A. He turns 27 in August and a transition to the bullpen may be necessary. ⚾ Former ninth-round pick **Packy Naughton** has added a little extra heat to his otherwise "soft-tossing southpaw with a change" profile, but feel for the curve remains on his to-do list. His name is Packy Naughton. ⚾ **Lyon Richardson** is a raw, athletic prospect with a ferocious delivery. He befuddled Low-A hitters as if Truthful Richardson was also on the mound with him and opponents could ask only one question. ⚾ [Pitcher Name] is a [insert year] [insert high round] Reds draft pick whose command isn't good enough to stick in the rotation but the big [right/left]-hander could become a contributor with a transition to the bullpen. We'll let you fill in those fields for **Tony Santillan**. ⚾ Thirty-year-old lefty relievers often end up stashed in Triple-A, and luckily for **Josh Smith** that means he can still occasionally hit the college bars he frequented at Wichita State. ⚾ After pitching in the majors two years in a row, the Reds left **Jackson Stephens** in Triple-A all year, where he threw 80 innings primarily as a reliever. Consider that a bad sign for his long-term job prospects. ⚾ It sure looks like **Tyler Thornburg**'s shoulder injuries have killed his career, but at least the Reds didn't have to give up Travis Shaw to find out.

Reds Prospects

The State of the System
Trades, injuries and stagnation leave the Reds system adrift somewhere in the bottom ten orgs.

The Top Ten

★ ★ ★ ★ *2020 Top 101 Prospect* **#59** ★ ★ ★ ★

1
Nick Lodolo   LHP   OFP: 60   ETA: 2020/21
Born: 02/05/98   Age: 22   Bats: L   Throws: L   Height: 6'6"   Weight: 202
Origin: Round 1, 2019 Draft (#7 overall)

The Report: The Pirates drafted Lodolo with the 41st choice of the 2016 draft, but the sides couldn't make a deal, and Lodolo enrolled at TCU where he toed the rubber for three years. As an amateur, he improved his K-rate each season until he topped out at 11.4 per nine his Junior year, when he also managed a 2.36 ERA. That performance was enough for the Reds to make the lefty the number seven overall pick in last year's draft. He's only thrown 18 ⅓ innings since his pro debut, but he's been impressive in that sample, striking out 30 without walking a single batter.

Lodolo is tall and lanky with very long limbs and a high waist. He has three plus pitches and he throws all of them for strikes. He fires from a true three-quarters arm slot and gets downhill, but can cut off his extension a bit. It's not the smoothest delivery out there, and he gets big time hand separation with his glove side getting in front early. His slider is consistent, sharp, and tough to pick up. He commands the slider and change well. Lodolo has good athleticism and controls his long frame well. His release point is incredibly consistent and it's virtually impossible to differentiate between the slider and fastball until it's too late for hitters.

As mentioned, Lodolo has thrown fewer than 20 professional innings, but it's almost impossible to be more impressive than he was in 2019 on the whole. He's an advanced college arm, and he isn't far off from the majors. I don't think it's probable, but I wouldn't be shocked if he is logging innings for the Reds if they are in contention in late in 2020. While he is in the minors, Lodolo starts are ones that you're going to want to get on your calendar.

Cincinnati Reds 2020

Variance: Medium. It's tough to be more impressive than Lodolo was in his small 2019 sample in the pros. He's a college lefty with an advanced feel for pitching. If for any reason he's unable to stick in the rotation, he will still be a difference maker out of the bullpen.

Mark Barry's Fantasy Take: Do you like guys with walk totals that are literally "LOL, no thanks"? Lodolo couldn't have been better in his first pro taste, and although all the standard caveats apply, I like him quite a bit and think he's an easy add into my top-75 or so.

2. Jose Garcia SS   OFP: 55   ETA: 2022
Born: 04/05/98   Age: 22   Bats: R   Throws: R   Height: 6'2"   Weight: 175
Origin: International Free Agent, 2017

The Report: The Reds gave Garcia a five million dollar bonus in the 2016-17 signing period. At the time the club was already over their international spending limit and were forced to pay a 100% tax on the signing. He then didn't play for the organization for almost a full year after, but Cincinnati threw him directly into full-season ball with Dayton in 2018. The first half of his stateside debut was rough, but Garcia has shown steady improvement since that point.

In last year's Reds top-10 list, Nathan Graham wrote that Garcia was poised for a breakout in 2019, and he couldn't have been more right. If you go to a game without knowing the rosters, Garcia is the one that will stand out immediately. He's long and lean with a high waist, and he's always going to be one of the most athletic players in any given game. Don't expect an elite defender at short, but he should finish as an above-average shortstop. He's smooth with good footwork and has a plus arm. He's a heady player with the glove and has plus speed on the basepaths. The swing is smooth and pretty, and the hit tool could end up plus, Garcis shows a solid approach and improving barrel control. Power is the biggest shortcoming in the profile, but it still projects to 10+ home runs. Don't expect a flashy player when he climbs the organizational ladder, but you can expect a prospect who does everything well without any weakness to his game.

Variance: Medium. Garcia projects to be a four tool contributor. He's young and hasn't escaped the low minors, but he's already displayed an ability to adjust and improve.

Mark Barry's Fantasy Take: I'm getting strong Cesar Hernandez-vibes from Garcia, which may seem like an unspectacular for the number-two prospect in an organization, but I swear, that's a compliment. He's not terribly close, though, and the low ceiling points to relevance in deeper formats or only leagues.

3. Tyler Stephenson C   OFP: 55   ETA: 2021
Born: 08/16/96   Age: 23   Bats: R   Throws: R   Height: 6'4"   Weight: 225
Origin: Round 1, 2015 Draft (#11 overall)

The Report: We now have two seasons of mostly healthy Tyler Stephenson, and the projection of a potential above-average everyday catcher has come more into focus. The track record of high pick prep catchers is abysmal, but after a successful season in Double-A, Stephenson looks like he might be able to buck the trends of his cohort. The main issue with high school backstops is just so much can go wrong given how long and complex the development track is. But for Stephenson the issues were simple, injuries marred his first few pro seasons, and he still hasn't caught 100 games in a season, which is slightly worrisome. He is on the large side for catcher, but moves well behind the plate. The catch and throw skills remain a bit rough, but projectable. Stephenson sets a big, quiet target, but can get a bit snatchy at the top and bottom of the zone. He has average arm strength, and a quick release for a big dude, but doesn't always get great carry on his throws. He has a good approach at the plate and despite some stiffness in the swing, projects for an 50/55 hit/power combination. If he can continue to refine his defense and stay on the field, he could be the first good prep catcher since...uh...Brian McCann?

Variance: High. Durability concerns still abound. If the hit tool plays down a bit up the ladder and takes some of the power with it, he might be more of a fringe starter.

Mark Barry's Fantasy Take: Don't look now, but we might be restarting the Tyler Stephenson Hype Train. Of course that train is sure to run off the tracks and spend countless days repairing its engine, but still. Despite his first-round pedigree, I wouldn't expect star-level performance from Stephenson, but he could flirt with a few fantasy top-10 seasons in his career.

4. Jonathan India 3B
OFP: 55   ETA: 2021
Born: 12/15/96   Age: 23   Bats: R   Throws: R   Height: 6'0"   Weight: 200
Origin: Round 1, 2018 Draft (#5 overall)

The Report: Calling a player "polished" isn't usually a pejorative, but in India's case it's a mixed blessing. He has an above-average glove at third with the arm to match. The glove there isn't so good that it's a carrying tool, mind you, and his performance at the plate in 2019 was uneven. India can struggle to strike a balance between patience and passivity, hit and power. He has above-average bat speed and feel for contact, but while he will rip one pull side on occasion, he tends to play more gap to gap, and it's not always the loudest contact. You'd like to give the offensive profile higher praise than "polished" at this point. India was drafted that high in the first round in part due to his "high floor," but what does that floor realistically look like? .270, plenty of walks, 10 HR, with a pretty good third base glove and the ability to play passable defense at a few other spots? There's more than that in the tank of course. And if that looks more like .280 with 15-20 home runs. You pencil him in every day in the second spot in your lineup. I'm just not fully convinced he gets there, and the lack of a carrying tool in this kind of profile is always a little concerning.

Variance: Medium. There's an obvious outline of a major leaguer here as you recite the tools, but when you look a little deeper, he doesn't play a premium defensive position and may not hit for a ton of power.

Mark Barry's Fantasy Take: I like India more than Garcia for fantasy purposes, but it's a similar high-floor, low-ceiling profile. India probably has better plate discipline, which gives him more room for error, but it sure would be nice if he could hit for *slightly* more power.

5. Hunter Greene   RHP

OFP: 60   ETA: 2022
Born: 08/06/99   Age: 20   Bats: R   Throws: R   Height: 6'4"   Weight: 215
Origin: Round 1, 2017 Draft (#2 overall)

The Report: I was in attendance for Hunter Greene's most recent start. The good news: He hit 100 on my gun on three consecutive pitches and ended the first with a 101 mph fastball. The bad news: he only threw two innings and the start took place on July 26th, 2018. It has been a long time since Greene saw game action. Technically he was removed from that start due to an "upset stomach", but it was later revealed that he was dealing with elbow issues. Finally in April of 2019 it was announced that he undergo Tommy John surgery after sustaining new UCL damage while throwing live batting practice.

The second overall pick in the 2017 amateur draft, Greene was very briefly a two-way prospect and received 30 rookie-level at-bats in his draft year. He has been solely a pitching prospect since and is heavily reliant on his fastball. When you have an 80 fastball though, you throw the 80 fastball. You never know how a player, especially someone so young and fastball dependent, is going to bounce back after Tommy John Surgery and what will be nearly two years removed from game action.

On last year's Reds list, we wrote that Greene was a "pitch-and-a-half prep arm," and even when healthy he was a fairly raw pitcher. He is blessed with elite arm speed and plus athleticism. It's going to take a while to get him up to speed when he returns to the mound, and even longer to develop into a pitcher from a thrower. Greene has incredible tools, so I certainly won't count him out, but he has thrown only 72 professional innings and is not as young as he once was.

Variance: Extreme. It was a volatile profile prior to his surgery, and even more so at this point. The Reds will give him every opportunity to develop and become a rotation piece in the majors. If he recoups his velocity he will have a job in a bullpen even if a starting role doesn't pan out.

Mark Barry's Fantasy Take: On one hand, it might be a good idea to see if Greene has any name value still left on the trade market. On the other hand, after going under the knife for Tommy John surgery last April, I'm not sure his value can get lower. I'd be ok moving on from the fireballer in shallower formats, but if you've waited this long to cut bait in deeper leagues, you might as well hang on and see how Greene looks upon his return to the bump.

6 **Tony Santillan   RHP**   OFP: 55   ETA: 2021
Born: 04/15/97   Age: 23   Bats: R   Throws: R   Height: 6'3"   Weight: 240
Origin: Round 2, 2015 Draft (#49 overall)

The Report: Santillan struggled more in his second time around the Southern League as his command and control went backwards. The stuff is still pretty solid, a low-90s fastball, a plus-flashing slider with two-plane action he commands well gloveside, and a potentially average change that will show some tumble. The change-up is 45ish enough now that it wouldn't be a bar to starting, but the command remains an issue. Santillan has a fairly simple, if uptempo, delivery, so there should be some command projection here, but he's also not the most athletic of moundsmen which can affect his mechanics and efficiency. I'd say the reliever risk has bumped a little bit as his command continues to scuffle, but it would be a potential plus fastball/slider combo in short bursts, so there are worse fallbacks. And there's still a decent chance he sorts the command issues out enough to be an innings-eating, if somewhat frustrating, mid-rotation starter.

Variance: Medium. The strikeout and walk rates went in the wrong direction in Double-A, and the reliever risk is up as well.

Mark Barry's Fantasy Take: Santillan's control seriously backed up this season, and I can't say it doesn't scare me a little. If you start from a middle-of-the-rotation upside there aren't a lot of fantasy-relevant places to fall to.

7 **Mariel Bautista   OF**   OFP: 55   ETA: 2023
Born: 10/15/97   Age: 22   Bats: R   Throws: R   Height: 6'3"   Weight: 194
Origin: International Free Agent, 2014

The Report: Bautista has been in the Reds system since being signed out of the Dominican Republic in 2014, but didn't make his way stateside until 2017, and he finally got his first taste of full-season ball in 2019. The Reds have been moving Bautista along with kid gloves. He put up big rookie-ball numbers in 2018, and it appeared he was primed to break out in 2019, but instead he floundered. Bautista was hot out of the gate [in 2019, but after the first month of the season he really struggled. In the second half of the season, he looked completely lost at the plate and showed a complete inability to lay off breaking stuff beneath the zone.

Bautista has a wiry frame which should benefit from added mass and strength as he ages. He is a tool shed with 70 speed and 60 raw power. He's quick-twitch and shows big-time athleticism. There is plus bat speed, and he handles pitches up in the zone like he was born to do it. He doesn't look out of place in center field, but he might be a better fit in a corner despite his speed. Bautista has all the gifts and tools needed to become an All-Star, but there is still a lot to piece together. He has been brought along slowly and is still raw for a 22-year-old. At some point there is going to need a swing reset and hit tool improvements. If he can retool to better handle the lower half the zone, he will be well on his way to realizing his potential. The Reds organization doesn't have the best player development track record in this regard, but there have been some positive changes there. Bautista has a long way to go, but the building blocks are in place.

Variance: Extreme. Bautista has yet to impress in full-season ball and is still extremely raw. The changes he needs to make are not minor. All the tools are there, but the clock is ticking.

Mark Barry's Fantasy Take: Bautista has been in the Reds organization for five seasons and and his ETA is 2023. Pass.

8 Jose Siri CF   OFP: 50   ETA: 2020/21
Born: 07/22/95   Age: 24   Bats: R   Throws: R   Height: 6'2"   Weight: 175
Origin: International Free Agent, 2012

The Report: Jose Siri the prospect gives me a bit of a headache. It's not from the stress of coming up with the evaluation—the strengths and weaknesses are both very apparent—but rather the process of them slotting him into a broader context, in this case the Reds system. Our OFP is supposed to be a 75th percentile outcome. But pegging Siri to a single number is imprecise to a degree that...well, gives me a headache. Admittedly there will be a degree of false precision in any single number ranking. There's a plethora of possibilities higher or lower for any prospect that we write up in these pages. We cover some of those in our variance section. For Siri, a short paragraph there feels insufficient.

He has tremendous bat speed, lightning-quick wrists that generate plus raw despite a still-lean frame. He's a plus runner and gets to his top gear quickly. He should end up above-average in center field. He has enough arm for right. Nothing particularly interesting so far. I mean the tools are interesting, but there's nothing unusual about a four-tool up-the-middle guy with hit tool questions. Siri won't be the first or last written up in these pages, but he feels like a series of discrete outcomes more than a continuum. It will either click or it doesn't. Some teams are using what I'd call "bucket reports" now, where you give a percentage likelihood for each outcome 2-8. And Siri feels like a prospect that is more likely to be a 7 or a 3 than a 5, which makes him particularly confounding to rank.

Variance: Still really high. He's 24 and struck out 32% of the time in Double-A. He didn't hit a home run in 112 PA in Triple-A with the coward ball (©Bradford William Davis). The tools are still there but as the years go by the lack of performance carries more and more weight.

Mark Barry's Fantasy Take: Look, I get it. It's hard to find steals. Having said that, if you strike out over a third of the time and walk at a clip less than nine percent, it's awfully hard snag those bags. Such is the Siri Dilemma (also, I feel like Vegas had a "Hey, Siri" reference at -350, so sorry to disappoint).

9. Michael Siani CF
OFP: 50 **ETA:** 2024
Born: 07/16/99 Age: 20 Bats: L Throws: L Height: 6'1" Weight: 188
Origin: Round 4, 2018 Draft (#109 overall)

The Report: The Reds made Siani their fourth round selection in the 2018 amateur draft as a Philadelphia prep. That Summer, he put up decent numbers in rookie ball, albeit without much in the way of power. So coming into last season, he was a trendy breakout candidate as he began his first year of full-season baseball. Well, Siani looked pretty bad to begin the year and awful in the middle of the season. He was too passive at the plate and struggled to make good contact. For most of 2019 he looked like he didn't belong in the level, but things turned around toward the end of the year—his passivity turned into patience and he started hitting more line drives.

The way Siani ended the year gave me some optimism about his chances to find his way to the big leagues at some point. He is a good defender with plus speed and should able to handle centerfield. He also has a plus-plus arm which would play anywhere on the grass and even stand out in right. The questions are at the plate. I don't expect him to develop much power. It's not there presently, and the body is close to mature. Siani has a compact swing and is short to the ball, but he still struggles with pitches up in the zone. The glove is going to play and if he's able find some consistency at the dish, he could blossom into a potential regular. At worst he is likely an up-and-down extra outfielder that will provide a club a solid glove that they can plug into any outfield position.

Variance: High. Siani is young and hasn't proven he can hit at this point. The glove should carry him up the organizational ladder and will keep his floor relatively high for a player with major offensive questions.

Mark Barry's Fantasy Take: Bret preached Siani's virtues in this spot last season, and hipster prospect hounds followed suit, touting him as a stealthy pickup. It didn't necessarily happen, but like Keith mentioned above, he started to find a rhythm toward the end of the season. As a guy that was really young for his level, that's definitely something to build on. Oh, he also stole 45 bases, which is nice. Toss Siani on the watch list, in shallower leagues, but he's rosterable in 300-prospect leagues.

10. Lyon Richardson RHP
OFP: 50 **ETA:** 2022
Born: 01/18/00 Age: 20 Bats: B Throws: R Height: 6'2" Weight: 192
Origin: Round 2, 2018 Draft (#47 overall)

The Report: Richardson plays with a chip on his shoulder and is going to challenge every single hitter he faces in his career. He pitches with a faster tempo than most, but does slow things down a bit when he puts a runner on base. He's athletic and repeats his delivery well despite some violence and herky-jerky mechanics. Richardson has a lightning quick move to first and should hold runners well. He typically works in the low-to-mid-90's, but has touched as high as 97. The changeup is inconsistent, but you'll see a good one on occasion. The breaking ball is a nice compliment to his fastball and will show sharp break when it's right. I expect Richardson is a reliever in the long run - he has the demeanor for it, and I don't think he'll ever have a consistent third pitch.

Variance: High—thus far he hasn't shown a great propensity for strikeouts, and with the bullpen a likely destination that is a bit of a concern. He hasn't thrown a professional pitch as a 20-year-old, so there is plenty of time for development, but the outcomes are wide-ranging.

Mark Barry's Fantasy Take: If Richardson is unlikely to ever develop a third pitch, his already low strikeout numbers make him unlikely to be fantasy relevant. As this was my last fantasy blurb for list season, I'd be Lyon if I said this wasn't a disappointing one to end on.

The Next Ten

11 **Stuart Fairchild   OF**
Born: 03/17/96   Age: 24   Bats: R   Throws: R   Height: 6'0"   Weight: 190
Origin: Round 2, 2017 Draft (#38 overall)

Fairchild has always had a broad collection of averagish tools, but his game could lack refinement at times. He'd get overly aggressive at the plate and try to tap into his merely average raw power, leading to Ks or poor quality of contact. It's an unorthodox swing, as he starts with his hands straight out over the plate and loads in and back, so there can be some stiffness and barrel control issues. But Fairchild has refined his approach and his above-average bat speed generates hard contact to all fields. He's found a decent balance between his hit and power tools now, and while he won't be a middle-of-the-order force, something like .260 and 15 home runs is perfectly plausible. Fairchild is an above-average runner that should stick in center, and has enough speed and arm to play any outfield spot. The bat might end up just short of an every day role, but Fairchild does a little of everything, and that should be enough to keep him employed in the majors for a while.

12 **Jameson Hannah   OF**
Born: 08/10/97   Age: 22   Bats: L   Throws: L   Height: 5'9"   Weight: 185
Origin: Round 2, 2018 Draft (#50 overall)

Acquired from the Athletics for a Tanner Roark rental, Hannah doesn't have a ton of upside due to some tweenerish tendencies in the profile, but he should have a productive major league career. He's a smaller guy with minimal stride and load, so it's very much a hit-over-power profile, although he can fire some balls into the gaps for you. There's an above-average hit tool, although the approach is still raw. Hannah shows good instincts in the outfield, although he may not have the sheer foot speed to play every day in center, and his arm is fringy enough to be a better fit in left. That said, he could handle all three spots in the outfield, hit a little bit, run a little bit, and there's a non-zero chance he develops enough pop to be a second-division starter type. The likely outcome here is fourth/bench outfielder though.

13. Tyler Callihan   2B/3B
Born: 06/22/00   Age: 20   Bats: L   Throws: R   Height: 6'1"   Weight: 205
Origin: Round 3, 2019 Draft (#85 overall)

Callihan slid to the third round of the draft from a late-first-round projection, and the Reds were more than happy to give him almost double slot to sign him away from South Carolina. He's a bat-first prospect with plus power projection, and if that all plays out you will find a spot in the field for him to stand. The Reds have tried him at both second and third base. Third base is a better fit, although his hands and transfer can be a bit rough, the actions somewhat mechanical. That is something you can smooth out, but I don't expect he'll ever be a good infield glove. You're here for the bat though, and Callihan offers a sweet, rotational lefty swing with plenty of bat speed and loft. The usual non-elite prep bat risks apply to the hit tool here, but there's above-average every day upside with 20+ home runs possible.

14. Rece Hinds   SS
Born: 09/05/00   Age: 19   Bats: R   Throws: R   Height: 6'4"   Weight: 215
Origin: Round 2, 2019 Draft (#49 overall)

Without much debate, Hinds possessed the best raw power of any prep prospect entering the 2019 draft. What tools he possesses beyond the pop is an entirely different debate. After winning several home run derbies in the summer showcase circuit, he was edged-out by Bobby Witt Jr. in the All-Star Game edition that is played in-between rounds of the MLB derby. While Witt was chosen second overall, Hinds was selected 47 picks later due to his one-dimensional profile. Playing for one of the most stacked high school teams in recent memory, he was relegated to the designated hitter role and spent time at both third base and the corner outfield spots because of his defensive liabilities. The arm is strong -- as is the theme for most of his skill-set -- but he lacks finesse and precision to handle a position like shortstop, and the max effort swinging may cause him trouble. On the bright side, with some refinement to his game, there is a lot of room for development in a young power-hitting archetype.

15. Joel Kuhnel   RHP
Born: 02/19/95   Age: 25   Bats: R   Throws: R   Height: 6'5"   Weight: 260
Origin: Round 11, 2016 Draft (#318 overall)

Kuhnel somewhat anonymously climbed the ranks of the Reds organization after converting to the bullpen following the 2016 draft. He's never dominated quite as much or rose quite as quickly as you'd expect from a college arm with a two-pitch mix as good as his fastball and slider. The fastball sits mid-90s and the four-seam has some giddy-up when he elevates it, and he'll throw a sinker down in the zone with decent run as well. The slider is a plus two-plane breaker in the upper-80s. Kuhnel works with an easy tempo and uses a short arm action that means hitters see the ball late. He lacks athleticism, but repeats well enough and fills up the zone, and he certainly doesn't lack for arm strength. A plus fastball/slider reliever is more common than it used to be, but you can still use on in the seventh or eighth inning.

16 Ryan Hendrix   RHP
Born: 12/16/94   Age: 25   Bats: R   Throws: R   Height: 6'3"   Weight: 185
Origin: Round 5, 2016 Draft (#138 overall)

Hendrix missed three months in the middle of the year due to injury, but when he was on the mound in Chattanooga, Southern League hitters struggled to deal with his fastball/curve combo. The fastball sits in the mid-90s and gets decent plane from the combination of Hendrix's height and high slot. The curve gets heavily-used, and it's not hard to see why he'd want to spam it—it's a power, 12-6 mid-80s breaker. He commands the hook better than the heater as well. Hendrix doesn't have much of a track record of throwing strikes, going all the way back to his time in the Texas A&M bullpen, so the wildness and lack of wiggle on the fastball may make him more of a middle reliever than late-inning fireman. Then again, the curve might be good enough that a high-leverage role is on the table regardless.

17 Packy Naughton   RHP
Born: 04/16/96   Age: 24   Bats: R   Throws: L   Height: 6'2"   Weight: 195
Origin: Round 9, 2017 Draft (#257 overall)

A somewhat generic college lefty when the Reds popped him late on Day 2 of the 2017 draft, Naughton has developed into a solid, if not spectacular pitching prospect. One of a growing group of young southpaws that emulate Cole Hamels, Naughton works primarily off a low-90s fastball and potential plus change. His fastball has ticked up into the low-90s since college, and he commands the pitch well enough to keep hitters from doing too much damage. The added velocity has helped separate it even further off his low-80s change. The cambio shows good fade and he commands it well as well. It will be his out pitch at higher levels as Naughton's curveball is below-average. Despite lacking premium stuff, Naughton handled Double-A in 2019 with aplomb. The profile is more backend starter or swingman without a breaking ball jump.

18 TJ Friedl   OF
Born: 08/14/95   Age: 24   Bats: L   Throws: L   Height: 5'10"   Weight: 180
Origin: Undrafted Free Agent, 2016

The story of how Friedl came to be a Red is a fun fact—he was signed as an undrafted free agent for $732,500 after no one realized he had been eligible for the 2016 draft—but his pro career turned out more or less how you'd expect a third or fourth round college outfielder's to go. It's more bench outfielder than starter; Friedl can play all three spots although his arm is a bit short for right and he has to grind it out in center. He won't hit for much power, but will be a pesky at-bat and get on base just enough to make himself useful if you have to start him for a month. Almost four years on from his signing, the circumstances add some nice color to what is a solid, if somewhat generic fourth outfielder prospect.

19 Vladimir Gutierrez   RHP
Born: 09/18/95   Age: 24   Bats: R   Throws: R   Height: 6'0"   Weight: 190
Origin: International Free Agent, 2016

You don't scout the stat line, but there really isn't any way to sugarcoat Guttierrez's 6+ ERA. Can you blame some of the 26 bombs in 137 Triple-A innings on the new baseball? Perhaps, but the horsehide isn't any different in the majors, and the intermittent fastball command issues, loopy curves that stay up, and flat change-ups bare some of the responsibility as well. Your management consultant will tell you not to mix praise in with criticism, and tt was a bad year, but nevertheless let's try to find some good in here. Gutierrez's low-90s fastball can get up to 95 and there's run when he's down in the zone with the pitch. If he is spotting the heater around the knees, batters will just beat it into the ground. A mid-to-upper-70s curve ball is inconsistent, and doesn't always have good late, downer action. It can be a bit humpy, but the best flash above-average. His low-80s change has plenty of velocity separation but can be flat with some tail, although he'll show you one with fade on occasion. Overall the profile was just far too hittable as a starter in the upper minors, but there might be something to be gained out of a move to the pen where Gutierrez can max out the fastball and try to throw the good version of the curve more.

20 Lorenzo Cedrola   OF
Born: 01/12/98   Age: 22   Bats: R   Throws: R   Height: 5'8"   Weight: 152
Origin: International Free Agent, 2015

And one more bench outfielder for the road. Cedrola has a bit more defensive value than Friedl—he's a bit better center fielder and has a stronger arm—but lacks even Freidl's power and physicality at the plate. Cedrola looks like he hasn't really grown out of his complex-league body, and while he controls the zone well enough, the swing can lack some oomph. It's really hard to be Ben Revere in 2020, and Cedrola likely isn't that good a hitter either. Well, maybe as good as the fourth outfielder version.

Personal Cheeseball

PC Jimmy Herget   RHP
Born: 09/09/93   Age: 26   Bats: R   Throws: R   Height: 6'3"   Weight: 170
Origin: Round 6, 2015 Draft (#175 overall)

He looks like the best over-30 rec league basketball player in your nearest medium-sized city (he's 26). He wears stirrups, of course. His mechanics wouldn't look out of place in the dead ball era, but he throws a heckuva lot harder than Kid Nichols. He's a sidearmer, naturally, but can get it up to 95. The slider's not bad either. It's a tough at-bat for righties, but the weird funk in his delivery means he might never throw enough strikes to keep him from logging a lot of miles between Louisville and Cincinnati. The aesthetics are different though and a reminder that baseball is a weird sport that you can occasionally bend to your will in odd ways.

Low Minors Sleeper

LMS Ivan Johnson   SS/2B
Born: 10/11/98   Age: 21   Bats: B   Throws: R   Height: 6'0"   Weight: 190
Origin: Round 4, 2019 Draft (#114 overall)

After going over slot for Hinds and Callihan, the Reds turned their attention to Johnson, a JuCo second baseman in Round 4. He's likely an inch or two shorter than his listed six-foot, but it's a solid, athletic frame. It's a well-balanced swing from both sides of the plate with solid bat control, but he might lack even an average offensive tool and is a better fit at second base than shortstop. Keep an eye on how the bat develops or doesn't in full-season ball.

Top Talents 25 and Under (as of 4/1/2020)

1. Nick Senzel
2. Nick Lodolo

3. Aristedes Aquino
4. Jose Garcia
5. Tyler Stephenson
6. Jonathan India
7. Hunter Greene
8. Tyler Mahle
9. Tony Santillan
10. Lucas Sims

For a team in theory opening its competitive window, the Reds sure are old on the "established major leaguer" side. Of 16 Reds producing at least a win in 2019, just two, Tyler Mahle and Aristedes Aquino, are 25 or younger. With value distrubuted by age of like an inverted bell curve, the Reds are going to have to thread a needle with their limited cohort who are both young and presently major league ready.

Part of the team's future success depends on what's around the next bend for Nick Senzel, who still has plenty of luster but also perhaps some twigs and dirt from barreling through the forest. Far outstripping rookie limits and approaching the qualified threshold in 2019, he middled on both the offensive (.742 OPS, 88 DRC+) and defensive sides. He's essentially without a position moving forward, with starting roles at his natural third base and adopted center field homes presumably blocked by Eugenio Suárez and new addition Shogo Akiyama. Still, there remain flashes of the player who was in 2016 the second overall pick, and the hope he might yet deliver on his star billing. As long as he is eligible for the 25U, there's room for dreaming on Senzel.

Aquino, too, gave plenty of reasons for Reds faithful to believe in him; exploding onto the scene with 11 home runs in his first 16 games. His 225 plate appearances as a whole pro-rated him as nearly a three-win player, and while it's unclear if the 25-year-old—eligible for this list by just three weeks—without a prospect pedigree is truly of that caliber, his small sample of a rookie campaign alone was more a showcase than many players ever get.

Mahle, meanwhile, has shown himself a much more average contributor: In 2019, his DRA- sat at 99, and that represented a step up after struggling in two previous majors stints. It's not an exciting profile, and as it stands now Maile is sixth in the rotation at best, but he has started 48 games across the past two seasons to replacement-level results, with indications he could do more in the future. Maile's not just some bit of junk mail, even if he's not what most Cincinnati fans have waited for.

Sims might appear a strange choice—in his last season of eligibility here, everyone's favorite simulated reality video game is the old man in the room by another measure: he was drafted all the way back in 2012 (in the first round).

Cincinnati Reds 2020

Finally making the move to the bullpen, he struck out nearly 12 per nine across 43 innings. To take the step beyond mid-leverage piece, the walks and home run rate need to come down, but as to the latter there will likely be a patch to the Sims (and everyone else) next season helping draw it down.

Part 3: Featured Articles

The Baseball Is Juiced (Again)

Robert Arthur

This article originally appeared at Baseball Prospectus on April 5, 2019.

It started when the normally reliable Chris Sale got lit up for three homers by the Mariners in the Red Sox's season opener. It was part of a record number of taters that flew on Opening Day, as starters from Sale to Zack Greinke were taken deep by the handful. Then Christian Yelich hit a home run in each of his first four games, tying yet another MLB record, this one for consecutive games with a dinger to start a season.

It didn't take long for fans and players to begin whispering and tweeting about the baseballs being juiced again. It's early yet for us to come to any definitive conclusion about the 2019 season, but preliminary data shows that the baseball has returned to its aerodynamic peak. Whether that means this season will smash home run records like 2017 did remains to be seen.

Before home run explosion over the last few years, no one worried too much about the baseball's air resistance. While MLB and Rawlings (the company that manufactures the official baseballs) kept track of dozens of metrics to make sure that the ball was consistent from month to month, they didn't measure drag.

But drag is incredibly important in determining how likely a hitter is to knock one out of the park. As baseballs become more aerodynamic, they travel further given a certain initial velocity. A deep fly ball that might have been caught at the warning track can instead go into the first row of the stands. A three percent change in drag coefficient can work to add about five feet to a well-hit fly ball, which can in turn increase home runs league wide by an astounding 10-15 percent.

It's possible to measure the aerodynamics of the baseball using the pitch-tracking radars currently in place in each MLB ballpark. By calculating the loss of speed from when the pitch is released to when it crosses the plate, you can directly measure the drag coefficient on the baseball. I first wrote about the role of decreasing drag in boosting home runs in 2017, and MLB's commission of scientists and statisticians later confirmed that the more aerodynamic baseballs in use that year were largely to blame for the spike in home runs. The same commission rejected some alternate hypotheses, like rising temperatures and a league-wide boost in launch angle pushing more balls over the fence.

The current era has featured some large fluctuations in drag coefficient, leading to first an explosion in 2016 and 2017, and then a dialing back of homers last year. Curious about the record-breaking home run tallies in the last few days, I used the same methodology to measure the aerodynamics of the baseballs so far in 2019.

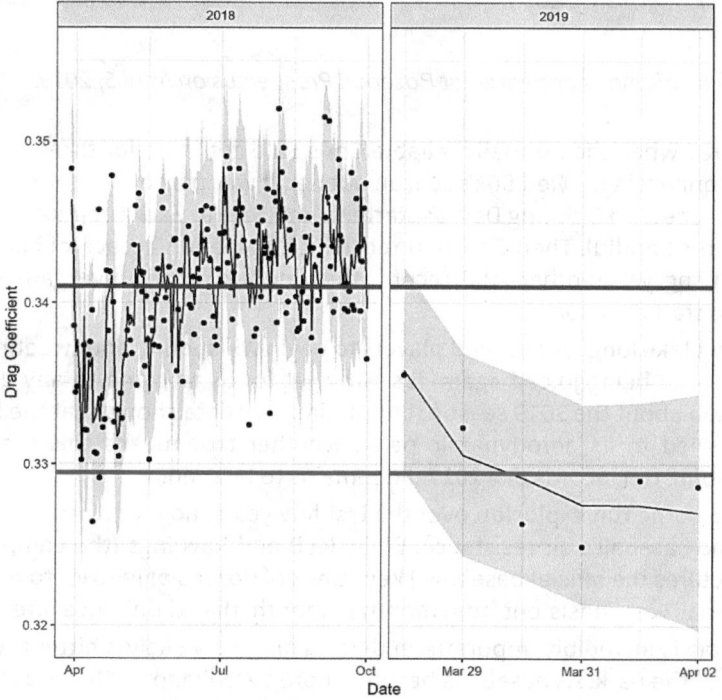

We're only a week into the 2019 season, but the drag numbers so far are among the lowest recorded in the last calendar year. With apologies for gory math, the current 2019 season average drag coefficient (the red line) would be below the 95 percent credible interval (the shaded area) for about nine-tenths of the 2018 season. (I used a Bayesian Random Walk model implemented in INLA to calculate these credible intervals, averaging the drag numbers in each game and adjusting for park.)

There were only a handful of six-day stretches in 2018 that had drag numbers below what we're seeing now, and most were in late June and early July. All of this means that 2019's data so far is quite a bit different than what we saw through most of last year.

These drag coefficients factor out the effects of temperature and air density, so they aren't a product of April cold. However, the numbers could be deceptive if the radars used to track pitches have changed from year to year. I consulted with some experts within baseball who were not aware of any specific modifications to the radar this year that could produce this pattern, but it's an important caveat of which to be aware.

On the one hand, it's only been six days, and we don't quite have the statistical basis to say that these drag coefficients are unprecedented compared to 2018. On the other hand, we've witnessed about 5,000 fastballs so far this season, so it's not as if our sample size is small. At least so far, the baseball has played like it's much more aerodynamic than it was last year. In fact, the current drag coefficient is really only comparable to 2017, when the baseballs were more aerodynamic than they had been in at least a decade.

It's not just fancy radar tracking indicating that the baseball is flying through the air more easily. The current number of home runs per game (as of this writing) is the highest it's been since the heady days of 2017, the year that teams and players broke dinger-related records everywhere you looked. That's especially remarkable considering that we're in what is typically the coldest part of the regular season, when lower temperatures and higher winds tend to suppress offense and keep balls in the air within the park. Comparing only from April to April, this year's rate of home runs per fly ball is even a little bit higher than it was in 2017.

With that said, the current measurements are no guarantee that 2019 will be another year of record-shattering homer hitting. The trouble with the drag measurements is that they are not consistent from June to August, from week to week, or even sometimes from day to day. Whether because of natural manufacturing variation or differences in the underlying supplies of cowhide and thread that go into the baseballs, drag has a tendency to fluctuate up and down over the course of a year. So the homers that fly in the first week of April wouldn't necessarily clear the fence a week later.

It's possible that this one-week drop in drag coefficient subsides and the baseball returns to its 2018 levels. On the other hand, it's almost equally probable that the ball becomes even more slippery and flies ever farther. Either way, it's clear that the baseball's air resistance is something to keep an eye on for the remainder of the 2019 season.

—*Robert Arthur is an author of Baseball Prospectus.*

The Moral Hazard of Playing It Safe

Craig Goldstein

This article originally appeared at Baseball Prospectus on August 6, 2019.

A couple days prior to the trade deadline, amidst a sea of tranquility posing as the lead up to the trade deadline, Bob Nightengale took to Twitter. Nightengale, who was probably wearing his pants backwards at the time, tweeted that MLB GMs were coming around on the idea that the unified trade deadline should be moved back from July 31 to August 15, so they could better assess their positions in the standings and whether they should buy or sell. To which I said:

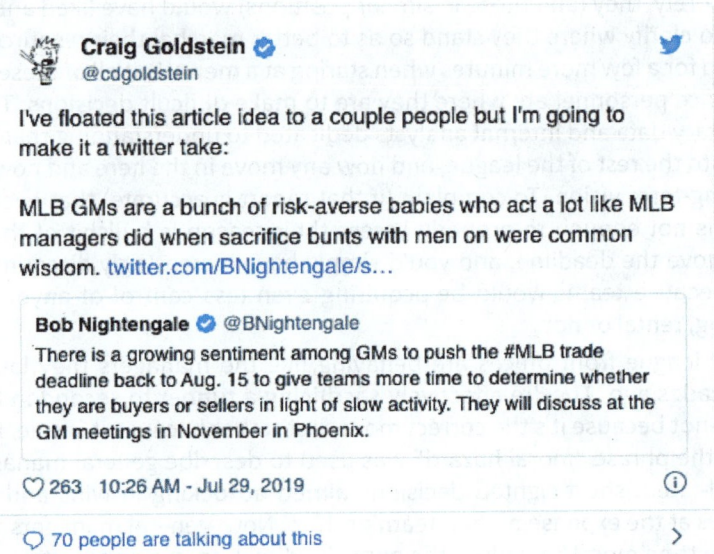

This might strike some as reductive and churlish. And it might be that, but it isn't really wrong, either. Jeff Quinton wrote a great piece discussing the environmental factors that enable front offices to avoid risk without upsetting the apple cart within their own fanbases. I don't believe that it goes far enough, however. His article gives us the proper framework through which to understand why these behaviors have been allowed to seep into front offices throughout the league. Understanding the reasons behind these actions are different from excusing them, though, and GMs should not be let off the hook for their non-competitive approach to the trade deadline (much less the offseason).

⚾ ⚾ ⚾

It's fair to say that fans as a group have rarely, if ever, been pro-player. It is also fair to say that in the time during and following the Moneyball revolution, the pendulum swung from fans who cared intensely about winning in the moment (and thus might be intolerant of a rebuilding approach) to fans who supported building a team that could compete throughout multiple seasons, viewing the playoffs as a crapshoot, with the thought that getting multiple bites at the apple was a better approach than taking a bigger bite in any one season.

There's nothing wrong with that approach, and I still find merit in that argument. However, it seems that the pendulum has swung too far in that direction. Teams are overvaluing some of the individual factors that make themselves long-term contenders rather than attempting to seize a championship when given the opportunity. It's a difficult needle to thread.

And surely, they (and those in similar positions) would have liked another two weeks to clarify where they stand so as to better marshal their resources. We've all asked for a few more minutes when staring at a menu. But all of these GMs and front office personnel are where they are to make difficult decisions. They have proprietary data and internal analysts dedicated to understanding their position relative to the rest of the league, and how any move in the here and now impacts their long-term vision. To complain (if that report is accurate) that over half the season is not enough to properly assess their season is bullshit of the highest order. Move the deadline, and you'd simply have increasingly discounted trade offers because teams would be acquiring even less control of anyone they're acquiring, rental or not.

Major league front offices are behaving like the managers they lampooned two decades ago. They're effectively sacrificing a runner to second in the ninth inning—not because it's the correct move, but rather because it is safe. It used to be that the phrase "moral hazard" was used to describe general managers who made ill-fated, short-sighted decisions aimed at locking in wins and securing their jobs at the expense of their team's future. Now, general managers are guilty of committing moral hazards in the opposite direction, playing it utterly safe and terrified of becoming scapegoats.

In lieu of bold action, they opt to pussyfoot around a current window of contention, choosing instead to play the long game and stack up years of control like they're blocks in a game of Jenga. GMs pass on signing quality players in free agency because the back-end of the deal might look bad, and because they might be able to squeeze out 70 percent of the production from a player who costs a tenth as much. That's a safer investment, too, because it's also hard to prove a negative—it's impossible to prove that Manny Machado would make the Mets a playoff team in 2019-2020, but it's easy to say that the back half of Robinson Cano's contract sucks. Owners, who rule over GM's jobs, are also humans with human brain processes that will always make the so-called albatross contract uglier than the road not taken.

These days, GMs are remembered for the bad deals they make and the surplus value they generate, not the acquisition of expensive, necessary talents that meet their market worth (or fall slightly short while still providing significant on-field value). And front offices know that one or two expensive misfires can cost them their jobs, no matter how many good deals they make.

No front office exemplifies this ethos more than the Toronto Blue Jays. General Manager Ross Atkins had this to say following the Blue Jays underwhelming trade deadline:

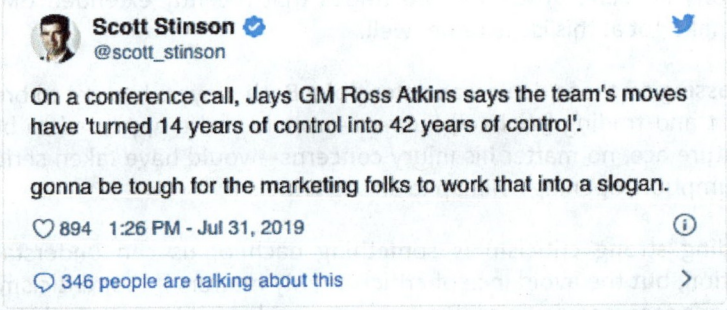

This is by no means the first time that an executive will cite years of control to justify their actions, which is often just another way of saying "don't look at what we got, look at how much we got of it." Atkins touts quantity to elide the discussion of quality—either, that of the players acquired, or those given up. Remember: the other teams presumably value years of control, too.

Atkins also had some thoughts to offer regarding free agents back in early 2018:

This ignores, of course, whether the player can create enough value in the front end of a contract to justify the longer term of a deal, and the decline that often occurs in the back end. It also ignores whether the player can fill a need the team requires and put them in a position to compete for and win a championship. But as teams seemingly avoid contention at all, where they might end up having to consider and later justify some of these tough decisions, we still see risk-averse approaches.

Anthony Fenech's article on two trades that recently extended GM Al Avila didn't make got at this issue rather well:

> Passing on those deals was defensible: Both players had yet to break out and trading [Michael] Fulmer—a pitcher who appeared to be a future ace, no matter his injury concerns—would have taken serious gumption, opening Avila up to strong criticism.

Avoiding strong criticism is something each of us can understand as a motivation, but the avoidance of criticism only matters if that criticism is valid. In Fulmer's case, shoving his injury concerns aside affects not only the years that the team controls him (he is currently missing a full season due to Tommy John surgery) but also the quality of those seasons, as his knee and elbow injuries combined to dampen his effectiveness even when healthy enough to pitch. But it was easy to present the then-current image of Fulmer as a top of the rotation pitcher who the team had under its domain for the next five seasons as something to build around. The status quo isn't nearly as often second-guessed as a decision that disrupts it.

MLB GMs are risk-averse to a fault. They are ivy-educated and consulting firm-approved, and yet they can't seem to avoid leaving wins on the table in their all-consuming lust for a non-existent $/WAR championship. They are supposed to zig when everyone else zags, and not merely pay lip service to the idea of zigging through a calculated PR plan built on convincing the fan base their approach is novel when it actually apes most of their competitors. Instead they've become far more concerned with making safe, accepted-by-the-new-common-wisdom decisions, such that our prior understanding of what a moral hazard is has become inverted.

I can't blame them entirely, and not only because of the reasons that Quinton illuminated in his article, but also because of the damage wrought by the introduction of the second wild card (WC2) spot. MLB's desire to have more teams in playoff contention has sparked anti-competitive behavior. Teams know now that they do not need to swing big as they assemble their roster because there is a good chance that a mediocre team can either catch fire and capture a division, or muddle along until they back into the WC2.

Simultaneously, the one-game playoff has neutered the WC1, putting an entire season on the flip of a coin like some sort of baseball-obsessed Anton Chigurh. While the one-game playoff makes sense as a way to increase the value of winning a division, it also means that if a front office doesn't like its chances of overcoming a behemoth like the Dodgers or Astros in the offseason, they have few incentives to chase glory. Similarly, the relative inaction in the NL Central at the trade deadline—despite a wide open division—can be explained by the idea that any high-variance investment could still result in only a wild card (or worse) result, given the mere two months left in the season to make an impact.

⚾ ⚾ ⚾

As stated at the top, we should not confuse reasons for excuses. The implementation of the second wild card is just one of many environmental factors that influence how each front office operates. I am convinced that it is one of the larger factors, but I am also convinced that organizations need to shed the yoke of "efficiency at all costs" so that they can instead pursue competition, as the spirit of the game intends. Until they do, we're all deadline losers. ■

—*Craig Goldstein is an author of Baseball Prospectus.*

Index of Names

Akiyama, Shogo	80	Hendrix, Ryan	97, 108
Alaniz, R.J.	97	Herget, Jimmy	110
Antone, Tejay	97	Hinds, Rece	107
Aquino, Aristides	18	Iglesias, Raisel	58
Barnhart, Tucker	20	India, Jonathan	85, 101
Bauer, Trevor	46	Jankowski, Travis	86
Bautista, Mariel	81, 103	Johnson, Ivan	110
Blandino, Alex	22	Jones, Nate	60
Bowman, Matt	97	Kuhnel, Joel	62, 107
Callihan, Tyler	96, 107	Lodolo, Nick	94, 99
Casali, Curt	24	Lorenzen, Michael	64
Castellanos, Nicholas	26	Mahle, Tyler	66
Castillo, Luis	48	Mella, Keury	97
Cedrola, Lorenzo	110	Miley, Wade	68
Colón, Christian	82	Minier, Braylin	87
De León, José	91	Moustakas, Mike	32
DeSclafani, Anthony	50	Naughton, Packy	97, 108
Dietrich, Derek	28	Reed, Cody	95
Duke, Zach	52	Richardson, Lyon	97, 105
Ervin, Phillip	83	Rodriguez, Alfredo	96
Fairchild, Stuart	96, 106	Romano, Sal	70
Farmer, Kyle	96	Santillan, Tony	97, 103
Friedl, TJ	84, 108	Schebler, Scott	34
Galvis, Freddy	30	Senzel, Nick	36
Garcia, Jose	96, 100	Shafer, Justin	72
Garrett, Amir	54	Siani, Mike	88, 105
Graterol, Juan	96	Sims, Lucas	74
Gray, Sonny	56	Siri, Jose	104
Greene, Hunter	92, 102	Smith, Josh	97
Gutierrez, Vladimir	93, 109	Stephens, Jackson	97
Hannah, Jameson	96, 106	Stephenson, Robert	76

Cincinnati Reds 2020

Stephenson, Tyler 89, 100
Strop, Pedro 78
Suárez, Eugenio 38
Sugilio, Andy 96
Thornburg, Tyler 97
Triana, Michel 90
VanMeter, Josh 40
Votto, Joey 42
Winker, Jesse 44